TO ENDURE – REKINDLED LOVE

By LARRY CALKINS

Larry Calkins

TO ENDURE

Cover Picture: The Boston Wharf by L. G. Calkins.

REKINDLED LOVE

By Larry Calkins
Stories Told by Travis Calkins

Copyright © 2022 Larry Calkins

All rights reserved.

ISBN: 978-1-7344718-2-3

This book is dedicated to:

My Father

B. Sep. 9, 1923; D. Feb. 5, 2009

My Grandparents

Grandmother B: Dec. 31, 1901 to D: Mar. 18, 1993
Grandfather B: June 11, 1881 to D: June 16, 1960

CONTENTS

	Acknowledgments	iv
	Prologue	1
1	My Great Grandparents and Grandparents	Pg #7
2	My Parents	Pg #17
3	The Honeymoon	Pg #31
4	My Birth	Pg #47
5	My Sister	Pg #55
6	Growing up in 1920s	Pg #63
7	The Great Depression	Pg #79
8	Sadness	Pg #97
9	Cumberland Island	Pg #111
10	Florida	Pg #121
11	Moses Brown	Pg #127
12	California	Pg #133
13	After the War	Pg #155
14	Investment Concerns	Pg #161
	Epilogue	Pg #169
	Reflections	Pg #173

TO ENDURE – REKINDLED LOVE

Acknowledgements

I would like to acknowledge the many people who helped me write, edit, and research this book.

First, a big thank you to my cousin, Phil, who became an inspiration and a mentor for this writing. He's an inspiration and encouragement to persevere, and his mind is still razor sharp. His critiques of this book became invaluable to the initial formation of this document.

I want to thank both my brothers, and sister who also gave suggestions. Tanny provided memories and valuable insight as to the core family values and reminded us of what life was like during the Depression. I want to thank Sandy, my cousin, who offered pictures and Margaret's Journal by Emma Bourne, described our grandmother's youth. Caroline, my other cousin, offered insight into genealogy and family history.

Stephanie Morris, my editor, amazed me with her insights into writing and offered her generosity when she understood the depth and meaning of this book. I appreciate all who expressed an interest in this project. I, also, thank the reader and hope you enjoy the result and find it inspiring.

Larry Calkins

Larry Calkins

Prologue

Dear Larry,

Thank you for helping tell my story. I'm glad you asked about my life and important family members in our history. I want you to know about them because I'd like you to understand the significant events that surrounded their everyday lives. You need to know the truth.

One life changing weekend for me in June 1987, your mother and I decided to attend a marriage encounter, a self-exploration event sponsored by our church. I was skeptical, but at the same time thought, "how bad could a church sponsored event be?" I thought my marriage could use some spicing up, and I talked your mother into going. After attending, I came away with a totally different perspective of not only my marriage, but also the family we created together. The future could be different; I could not change the past.

Your mother and I learned how to love each other better, but also I came away with a strong sense that the children we raised bound us together in a strong bond and my family mattered. I don't mean just your mother and you kids, but our whole extended family. The richness of all our family—both the good and the bad—bound us together, and we should make the best of it. It was the bond of matrimony that gave us not one but two families that we could embrace, or not. But, if we did, it could become powerful and enriching. It's a good training ground for the rest of your life, for anyone and everyone you encounter, as well as how to love humanity; for in a sense, we are all siblings, cousins, aunts or uncles in many ways.

For this reason, I want to explain more in depth who our family members are; unvarnished and as true as I can be to their rich legacy. It is one that we can be proud of, but at the same time can learn from the mistakes they made and how they coped with tragedies which were mostly out of their control.

Despite the struggles I had growing up, it easy compared to many families during The Great Depression. Our family started with money and reputation. The character of our family helped us tremendously because we held tightly to family connections and friends to see us through the Depression.

I have attached our family tree showing three generations and the relationships between our family members. I found I love my family and the heritage they built for us. I hope you treasure the stories of your legacy as much as I do and are able to preserve it.

With much Love,

Dad

TO ENDURE – REKINDLED LOVE

Larry Calkins

MY FAMILY

Travis Calkins
B: Sept 1923 D: Feb 2009
Brother of: Sarah
Married to: Billie Jeanne (1)
   Lucia (2)
Father of: Larry Calkins

Parents

Giles Calkins
B: Jun 1881 D: Jun 1960

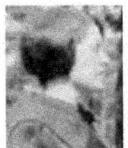

Margaret Calkins
B: Dec 1901 D: Mar 1993

Author's note: My name is Larry Calkins and Travis was my father. He related countless stories and wanted me to pass them on. This book contains the stories he told and the book is written from his perspective. I also feel that it is important to share not only his memories but the legacy of those who went before.

TO ENDURE – REKINDLED LOVE

TREE

Grandparents

Travis Giles Calkins
B: Mar 1846 D: Dec 1916

Ida May Calkins
B: Nov 1855 D: Apr 1936

Edwin Bourne
B: Jul 1861 D: Jun 1938

Emma Bourne
B: Sept 1867 D: Mar 1949

TO ENDURE
REKINDLED LOVE

Chapter 1 – My Maternal Great Grandparents and Grandparents -The Bournes

Charles Taber, born 20 April 1822; Died 17 November 1887: My great grandfather, Charles began his education at the Friends' School in Providence, Rhode Island. He went on to graduate from Haverford College in Pennsylvania at about eighteen after a flattering record of academic achievement and winning scholarships to meet his educational goals.

Charles' father, William C. Taber, started in the book business in New Bedford. In 1843, Charles learned his father's business and, when William retired in 1849, Charles formed the firm Charles Taber & Co.

Sarah Jane Howland, born 24 February 1832; died 17 June 1905: Charles married Sarah Jane, my great grandmother, on March 31, 1853. They raised five children to adulthood. A sixth child known as "Fanny, the angel of the family", died in childhood. The Tabers and Howlands came from a long line of Quakers. Charles' lineage could be traced back to the early Americas, and before that to royalty in England.

With the help of his brothers, the book business expanded to two book and stationary stores and in 1862, the company started manufacturing photographs at Number 6 Water Street. Later, in 1881, Charles' eldest sons, Charles M. and Frederic, joined their father in business becoming his partners.

Charles M. Taber born 7 February 1856, died 27 February 1915; and Frederic Taber born 28 September 1856, died 25 December 1930: Charles M. and Frederic joined their father in the thriving book and photography business, slowly taking more responsibility for the business until he passed in 1887. Charles M. took on the majority of the responsibility of his father's business.

By 1889, Charles Taber & Co. had five buildings that manufactured ambroytypes, or photographs on glass, and artotypes, engravings and etchings. The Company became one of the first to market the face of Elizabeth Fry[1], the English philanthropist and a member of the Society of Friends. The Society of Friends, a Quaker religious organization, members promoted ideas such as prison reform and the abolition of slavery in the 19th Century Charles Taber & Co. became internationally known, selling these and other images worldwide and

---

[1] Elizabeth Fry took up plain language and traditional dress of the Quakers in 1798 and devoted herself to helping the sick and needy. She addressed the House of Commons in England about prison conditions in 1818 and became a well-known personality in prison reform. Young Queen Victoria of England became a great admirer of Fry. Elizabeth Fry passed away in 1845, but her prison reform and opposition to the death penalty informs current prison reform efforts today. https://www.evangelicalsforsocialaction.org/heroes-of-the-faith/heroes-of-the-faith-elizabeth-fry/

TO ENDURE – REKINDLED LOVE

made the company famous.

During this time, New Bedford became a city of the arts. An 1889 book, entitled "Board of Trade," begins with a chapter on "Art Industries" that leads with Charles Taber & Company. The company moved into fine art reproductions, producing the "finest engravings and etchings." They manufactured their own frames.[2]

> The firm of Charles Taber & Company pioneered the art manufacturing industry in this country. Today, it is the largest of its kind, the annual product aggregating nearly a half million dollars in value.

In 1893, the company changed its name to Taber Art Company. Then, in 1897, the firm merged into the Taber Prang Art Company[3].

Emma Taber my Grandmother

Emma Taber born 17 September 1867; died 17 March 1949: Emma Taber, my grandmother, was the youngest of five living siblings, who admired her older brothers Charles M. and Frederic. She also had two older sisters, Elizabeth Taber, and Sarah Howland Taber. While her older brothers continued the family business in the 1890s, Emma took pleasure in her family's community standing and promoted it, in her own way, by helping in church and community events.

She developed into a delightful, charming, quick-witted, strong-willed young woman. She became active in the Unitarian Church

---

[2] *"Board of Trade" 1889, New Bedford, Art Industries Chapter*

[3] *Courtesy of my niece, Caroline Pomeroy.*

keeping her Quaker values as did many of her immediate family members.

Emma learned to be thrifty and, some may say, miserly from her Quaker roots. But, she remained very much a lady with proper manners and held a strong command of her household. Emma's piercing steely-blue eyes, strong jawline, well-proportioned face were only part of her beauty. Her striking features, coupled with her charm, attracted men from all walks of life. Still, she remained particular about the type of man she wanted to marry.

Great-uncle Frederic Taber, Emma's older brother and simply known to me as Uncle Fred, became a charter Board Member of the New Bedford Safe Deposit and Trust Company in 1887 while still helping his older brother Charles with the Charles Taber & Co. Uncle Fred, eventually became the Bank President[4] as well as Chair of the Board at the Bank. With the help of his brother and father's money, Uncle Fred had a number of other business ventures in New Bedford including the Taber Textile Mills, established in 1906 in Northern New Bedford. Fred became President of that Mill as well. But with more demands on his time, he needed a right hand man to help run

Emma's Brother Fred Taber

---

[4] The opportunity for banking came from many business adventures in New Bedford. Fishing, historically and today, continues to be the livelihood of many a New Bedfordite. The whaling industry from 1780 through the mid-1800 produced whale oil as the predominant energy source lighting lanterns throughout the new world. Later petroleum became more abundant. Crude oil shipped to New Bedford from Pennsylvania became refined into usable oil and petroleum distillates.

TO ENDURE – REKINDLED LOVE

the bank.

Edwin Bourne became that man for many years.

> Uncle Fred didn't know our grandfather Bourne well, but Grandfather Bourne ran away from home as a teenager to become a cowboy out west. He then morphed into a frontier banker with a partner named Mack. He and Mack, at one point, had to defend the bank with their guns, shooting out the windows at the bandits.
>
> When Grandfather came back to New Bedford, Uncle Fred was quite successful sitting on top of Taber Mills, Chairman of Bank, etc. and his young son was not in a position to take over the mill. But, he had two problems. First, he had this sister, Emma, at home, unmarried, who was getting on in years and about to become a spinster. (I speculate she was about 29.) Second there was the problem of succession at the bank. He felt nobody could take over after their father died.
>
> Then from out of the west—I mean the Wild West —came this energetic and experienced cowboy, turned banker, who became the ideal candidate. Furthermore, Grandfather came from a good, well-known New Bedford family. It solved both problems; a suitor for Emma and a banker who had the grit to run a bank.
>
> *Sarah Calkins Palmer (my sister)*

Edwin Bourne born 22 July 1861; died June 1938: Edwin W., my grandfather, was born in New Bedford. After a youthful excursion into the west, he returned to settle down. His charm and self-confidence helped create his reputation as an up and coming citizen in a small town. His hair parted in the middle with a full mustache accented his handsome features, giving him an aura of importance.

Standish Bourne, Edwin's older brother and a prominent auctioneer in New Bedford was also on the Board of the "New Bedford Safe Deposit and Trust Company". Standish related a story about how Edwin went out west and fought off would be bank robbers. Edwin applied for the job of a cashier. His brother's story, recommendation, and along with his experience as a clerk and bookkeeper in Boston helped convince the Board. Edwin impressed Uncle Fred, and the Board hired him.

Edwin, a local boy, had become a New Bedford cashier at a prominent bank in New Bedford. His boss, John W. Macomber, the bank's President[5] at the time, connected well with the youthful and energetic Edwin Bourne. Edwin made his living from persuading his banking patrons that he could be trustworthy and would protect their money at all costs. Quakers owned the Bank, and Quakers had enjoyed a long history of trustworthiness and faithfulness with their clients. They made excellent bankers because of their extraordinary care and thriftiness.

In the 1890's, Emma met Edwin when she was introduced by Uncle Fred, who felt responsible for his younger unmarried sister. Uncle Fred, was delighted when Emma chose Edwin and married him on October 20, 1898.

Edwin and Emma raised a family of four children; **Margaret**, my mother, was the second oldest and the only girl born December 1901. Margaret's older brother **Joe** was born February 1900. Her younger brothers were **Rich** born July 1903; and **Edwin Junior** born June 1905. My grandparents raised their family in a modest but spacious, two story, New England-style home on Arnold Place in New Bedford. The three

---

[5] John Macomber remained Bank President until 1899; Previously, he managed the New Bedford Cordage Company, and had a hearty and energetic manner; "The History of New Bedford", Volume I, Zephaniah W. Pease, Editor, Lewis Historical Publishing Company, New York 1918.

TO ENDURE – REKINDLED LOVE

boys and Margaret had everything they needed.

Edwin, my grandfather, had a good and steady career at Uncle Fred's bank.[6] His formal career started and ended at the bank. Uncle Fred remained on the Board, but also became president after Macomber retired. Edwin walked the ten to fifteen-minute walk down the cobblestone streets to the bank every day. He likely walked down Union Street then crossed Seventh Street near the famous Ricketson's house at Union and Seventh Street[7], turned down Pleasant Street, passed the New Bedford Library, and then down Williams street.

Edwin enjoyed a wealthy environment after 1898 until around 1918 and invested in real-estate and southeast Massachusetts economy, especially in the areas surrounding New Bedford. Family rumor is that Grandfather Bourne purchased most of the town of Nonquitt, southwest of South Dartmouth, and some homes in Fairhaven across the Acushnet River from New Bedford.

In 1918, Uncle Fred became overwhelmed with his other ventures and wanted to remain Chairman of the Bank's Board. So, in 1919, he promoted Edwin to President of the Bank to run day-to-day operations. Edwin proudly proclaimed his presidency to friends, new

---

[6] the New Bedford Safe Deposit and Trust Company: was located at 61 Williams Street in New Bedford

[7] On Union Street across from Seventh Street stood the home of Joseph Ricketson Sr., who, with the help of William C. Taber, meet Frederick Douglass and his wife on the Newport wharfs and brought them to New Bedford. Here, at 179 Union Street, Ricketson's son Joseph housed the famed Henry "Box" Brown. Brown had escaped "packed up a box and sent on express from Richmond to Philadelphia marked 'this side up' but someone turned it upside down and nearly killed him." From there Brown made it to New Bedford according to Ricketson. National Park Service leaflet entitled "A Near Approach to Freedom." www.nps.gov/nebe and www.cr.nps.gov/ugrr

Larry Calkins

acquaintances, and family members as if he had been president throughout his stay at the bank.

In 1920 and 1921, a depression hit the country after a period of wartime prosperity between 1914 and 1918.[8] In August 1921, the United States economy started to pick up, ushering in the roaring twenties.

Edwin remained bank President until 1921, but it remains unclear why Edwin stopped being President, and his time at the bank ended. There are no records of him continuing at New Bedford Safe Deposit and Trust Company or any other bank as President. Emma had also pointed out that 1921 turned out to be a poor year for the family financially[9].

At 60 years old, Edwin should have been too young to fully retire, but he retained his assets and his investments. In order to sustain himself during his retirement years, he sold off his real estate.

***

In the late 19th century, the textile industry gained steam producing fabrics from cotton and silk. Textile Mills flourished in the

---

[8] The Depression of 1920-21 turned into a sharp deflationary recession in the United States and other countries. It lasted until July 1921. It became characterized by extreme deflation - References: U.S. Business Cycle Expansions and Contractions, National Bureau of Economic Research, September 22, 2008.

[9] Around 1921, the New Bedford Textile Trust Company planned a merger with The New Bedford Safe Deposit and Trust Company on April 15, 1922. The merger was approved with a commitment for a new bank building to be built on Pleasant and Williams Street. The bank was renamed The Safe Deposit National Bank. In 1922, Mr. Cook became President of the bank and Cook remained President until the late 1940's.

TO ENDURE – REKINDLED LOVE

area. Money flowed through New Bedford due to these industry and banks provided a secure place to keep and invest that money. Both Fred and Edwin kept close ties with the textile industry to keep their bank finances in good order.

The industries also brought immigrants and others into New Bedford. Some of those coming to the area escaped slavery or worked in the whaling industry. New Bedford, in the late 18th century, enticed the Portuguese and Cape Verdean immigrants forming the backbone of the whaling industry. As merchandise from foreign lands entered New Bedford from the high seas, seamen from many different regions of the world came to New Bedford and settled in the area.

As early as 1780, Quaker abolitionists and the African Methodist Episcopal Church began helping slaves escape from the south. Harriet Tubman and John Brown, known as conductors, notably helped slaves escape the south to move north. In the 1840s, The Underground Railroad brought runaway slaves to the New Bedford area and local abolitionists, known as stationmasters, protected them. Frederick Douglass commented on coming to New Bedford because Margaret's great-grandfather, William C. Taber, and a friend and fellow Quaker suggested Douglass share a stage coach with them.[10]

---

[10] My niece, suggested William C. Taber as identified in Frederick Douglass' book "My Escape from Slavery" must have been William Congdon Taber, Margaret's great grandfather. Douglass states in the book that he was fortunate that a Quaker gentleman, William C. Taber, understood his situation and, in a quiet way said: "Thee get in." Douglass and his companions were soon on our way to their new home.

Larry Calkins

TO ENDURE – REKINDLED LOVE

Chapter 2 - My Parents

My mother, Margaret Bourne, born in New Bedford, Massachusetts came from old New England families with a Quaker pedigree going back, as she proudly proclaimed, "to the Mayflower."

My grandmother, Emma, prepared a journal of Margaret's early life. In it, she chronicled Margaret's birth.

> Little Margaret Howland Bourne came very nearly being a New Year's present – but not quite – however, she brought the Old Year of 1901 to a very happy close by entering our little family that evening at 7:30. Unlike Joe *(her older brother by 1 year)*, she was a little ... baby – only a little over six pounds with quantities of black hair, very dark blue eyes which will turn dark probably later. But we loved her from the very start, for she was a little daughter and had cause to make our family complete – a little boy and a little girl. ...
>
> Here, like yesterday it seems, when after a tiresome day of suffering, they laid a wee baby girl in my ready arms and I gave her the means for subsistence – how as she grew I loved her more and more. For this little girl was like a timid fawn. She clang to me everywhere and always.
>
> She was so shy and her very shyness made her love me, and me love her naturally all the more. How I watched each development, each new phase, so proud and so happy to have a dear little daughter to love.
>
> *Emma Bourne (My Maternal Grandmother), from her Journal.*

Margaret attended Friends Academy, a Quaker school in New Bedford, and graduated from Lincoln School of Providence, Rhode Island. She then attended Fannie Farmer's cooking school in Boston in preparation for a career as a housewife. Yet, she had ambitions of seeing the world and doing exciting things outside of New Bedford.

When Margaret graduated from Lincoln School, Emma intended to celebrate Margaret's graduation with a dance. Unfortunately, the prosperous war years of 1914-1918 turned to a depression in 1921, which only amplified the financial hardships that Edwin faced and he did not feel up to putting on the celebration. Instead, Emma's brother, Fred, stepped in and put on a large "Tea" in Margaret's honor. The Tea "did everything that money could do" including throw a beautiful party, according to Emma.

In November 1920, Margaret's father met a young man at his men's club, named Peter McMickle, who Margaret's father enjoyed the company of very much. Mr. McMickle stayed with the family during the summer of 1921. Since the financial difficulties of at this time prevented them from continuing the services of a maid, Margaret still living at home helped her mother with homemaking duties.

Margaret helped her mother feed four hungry men that included her brothers: Joe, who came home from college, and Edwin Jr., who just finished high school, as well as Edwin senior, and his friend Peter. Some said Edwin senior had Peter in mind to marry his only daughter.

TO ENDURE – REKINDLED LOVE

> Toward the end of winter, father met a man, Peter McMickle, at the Club who was destined to spend much time here for the following summer – as father seemed to enjoy his companionship very much. Again, we had no maid for many months and Margaret and I catered to the appetites of hungry men. Richard was on a cruise for part of the summer but Standish and Edwin were at home.
>
> It seems we're on Edwin's *("E," Emma and Edwin Senior's son)* account to put him on an entirely different school and so Margaret, Edwin and I left home on October 1, 1921 and spent that winter in Boston, where Edwin went to the Woodart Institute for one year course in carpentry – with the ultimate result of finding his own latest powers as well as to withdraw for a while from discouraging influences. We found ourselves very comfortably and happily settled at Miss Cattin's. Every part, every plan seemed to dove-tail in with every other part and plan, that not in a moment did I feel that we had made a mistake.
>
> In the meantime, Margaret took the six month course of housekeeping at Miss Farmer's cooking school. We planned for much work and not too much play. The winter would have gone down on record as such – busy. Happy and not too regretful had not George Gifford not invited Margaret to a dance where she met a man destine to become her husband before another year rolled around.
>
> *Emma Taber Bourne*

That autumn, Emma, Margaret and Edwin Jr. (Emma and Edwin senior's son) left New Bedford for Boston so young Edwin could attend Carpentry School and Margaret could attend Fannie Farmer's Cooking School. Emma stated a side benefit included they could leave New Bedford to "withdraw for a while from discouraging influences."

***

Larry Calkins

Margaret, at twenty years of age, had jet black hair and a smile that showed her impish ways. She stood about 5' 6" tall with a slender figure at about 125 lbs. Her immediate family and closest childhood friends called her "Kitty," but most used her more formal name, "Margaret," to show respect. Full of fun, Margaret could talk anyone's ear off. Her keen sense of self and her heritage pointed to the well-respected name of Taber and Bourne[11] showing her status, not only in New Bedford, but dating back to the early years in America. She had a persuasive nature and her love of life involved an adventurous spirit that emphasized her desire to see the world.

Margaret Bourne
My Mother

Although Margaret relished a zest for adventure and high-jinx, she innately became a proper young lady as Emma, her mother, taught Margaret New England manners and etiquette. She sustained a formal approach to her life with the Quaker influence of thrift. At the same time, she kept high spirits and could outwit anyone who challenged her. She always considered herself part of high society. Although there is some evidence to suggest her lineage had royal blood, it trailed down a long line of succession on her mother's side to King Alfred (the Great), King of Wessex, who died in 899 A.D. King Alfred had a reputation as a

---

[11] Margaret is distantly related to Myles Standish on her father's side through Lucy Standish Bourne, her paternal grandmother, and likely related to John Howland through Sarah Jane Howland Taber, her maternal grandmother. Both Myles and John sailed to Plymouth from England on the Mayflower. The pilgrims hired Myles Standish, an English military officer, to accompany them on the Mayflower to the Plymouth colony in current day Massachusetts. John Howland was an indentured servant and later a personal secretary to Governor John Carver becoming a free man in 1626.

TO ENDURE – REKINDLED LOVE

learned and merciful man with a level-headed nature.

One evening in 1922, Margaret went with friends to a dance at Harvard College. By chance, a Midwestern businessman named Giles Calkins, who had some Harvard connections, attended the same dance. He noticed that the pretty girl from New Bedford seemed relatively free of serious attachments, and he asked her to dance several times. Although younger than he, she seemed sophisticated and self-assured. He became more than a little interested in her.

> Mother teased, "Did you know, I'm related to John Howland on my mother's side? In fact, Howland is my middle name." When asked about John Howland, she joked, "You remember, [John] the guy who fell off the Mayflower." She laughed and simultaneously teeter one way and then the other. She implied he acted out of sheer clumsiness. She always smiled broadly as she retold this story.
>
> *Sarah, my sister*

Giles, twenty years her senior, was an accomplished artist, engineer, and salesman by the time he met Margaret. After high school, he attended the new Chicago Art Institute, a prestigious art school, located near downtown Chicago. Giles then attended Yale in New Haven, Connecticut, receiving a degree in Metallurgical Engineering. He lived in both New England and Chicago and traveled to points as far west as Arizona.

For 14 years, until 1920, Giles had worked in Chicago for a firm called Rogers, Brown and Company. When Margaret and he met, he had just begun working for a New York firm called Crocker Brothers where he sold pig iron, ferrous alloys and coke to the New England area steel mills. His offices were located on Milk Street in Boston.

Larry Calkins

Giles, my father, stood tall and had handsome features for an older gentleman at 39 years old. He had experienced wild adventures, but now he wanted to settle down, find someone he could share his life with and raise a family. He had been engaged to other women before. But either he or his fiancé would break off the engagements. No one seemed quite right for him until Margaret came along.

Giles, the oldest of three siblings, and the only boy, valued being adored by his younger sisters. He took his role as head of the family of origin seriously, offering compassion, a listening ear and advice to his sisters when needed.

Giles's care and kindness showed through in every aspect of his demeanor and in almost every situation. His gentleness, like his father, contrasted against his self-assurance and commanded life, as if he knew his abilities at every step of the way. His dark eyes studied the person he talked to, trying to ascertain the context behind the words. If anything, he sometimes focused too hard or became too intense, but he maintained his thoughtfulness. He thought of others and their well-being before thinking of his own needs.

The true nature of his character showed he enjoyed people, took life seriously and adsorbed all of life's great beauty and details. He kept the same intense attention when working on his artwork. When it came to his artwork, he could indulge himself. He would quietly go into another state of mind so he could focus on the details of his subject.[12]

---

[12] For instance, the picture he drew of me in my youth, showed every strand of hair, and it detailed my eyes, nose and mouth. It could have been mistaken for a photograph had you not seen the pencil marks not been visible on the paper.

TO ENDURE – REKINDLED LOVE

Giles said he came from Chicago, but, more accurately, he came from Evanston, Illinois, where his parents raised him. Once he moved to Chicago for art school, he explored his love of drawing and took a small step to see a larger world. Even then, he knew art could not be a full-time career choice. He was confident in his artistic talent, but he also knew he couldn't rely upon his art to make a decent living. He applied and immediately was accepted to Yale to explore metallurgical engineering.

Giles dressed impeccably in double breasted suits of the era, but he could just as easily relax in a pair of trousers when he enjoyed time with his friends. Around the house, he dressed in nice work clothes for menial labor or could dress to fit into a rough and tumble environment with other cow pokes. His stubby fingers and fat thumb could grip with a strong hardy handshake. Those hands suited him well as he etched, drew, and addressed a multitude of tasks. Even though his hands did not appear dainty, they had a gentle touch and moved with dexterous precision to paint or etch the detail he needed in his drawings and etchings.

> Margaret was gorgeous and popular, and could have had plenty of others if she had wanted. As to why she was smitten with Giles, Giles was a little older and drove a big flashy car and seemed to have lots of money, but nobody knew him.
>
> He was not from New Bedford, where everybody knew everybody else and there were a lot of intermarrying. As an example, my mother and father were distant cousins, and I think Cousin Helen, F. H.'s (young Frederic) wife's maiden name was Bourne so we were told she became a 'double cousin'. Maybe being 'from away' is exactly why Margaret fell for him.
>
> *(Tanny, my cousin, about Sarah's age)*

Giles seemed much worldlier than Margaret, and she became both intrigued and a little frightened of his abilities and background. The following week after their chance meeting at the dance, Giles went to New Bedford and knocked on her door.

Margaret told the story, "Giles came to the door to call on me. As my mother answered the door, I hid and cowered behind the stove in the kitchen. For some reason, I didn't want him to see me right away, like a little school girl." Still, his debonair demeanor, handsome physique, and his way with words swept her off her feet.

Emma in her journal describes Giles. Emma states there were many potential suitors that came to Margaret's door, and she viewed Giles as just one of many.

Margaret's family had serious reservations about their relationship. Giles settled in Massachusetts after Chicago. He could have been a foreigner in their eyes with his fancy car and Chicago credentials. At that time, perhaps more than now, outsiders and people of unknown family origin had difficulty breaking into the society of the highly suspicious New England natives. Her parents considered the impulsive leap into a quick marriage by their only daughter irresponsible. To say the least, my grandfather, Edwin, expressed significant dissatisfaction with my mother's choice. If it weren't for Margaret's insistence she marry him, it would have been unacceptable and even unthinkable. Although he had someone else in mind for her to marry, he could only accept her choice after he witnessed his daughter's strong determination. Emma appeared more circumspect, realizing there were things out of her control. She only wanted the best for her daughter.

TO ENDURE – REKINDLED LOVE

Margaret could not be talked out of it. She was insistent that she marry Giles, despite her family's reluctance. She argued that he expressed himself well and had promise to provide her with a good family income. Besides that, he'd attended the prestigious Art Institute of Chicago, secured an engineering degree from Yale, and told stories of his western travels that she loved. She expected her father to eventually like him, because he, too, had youthful western adventures. She couldn't wait to participate in Giles's future adventures. She wanted to try something new, especially if it meant getting out of New Bedford.

> It was for one of those things in which fate decrees, and one, especially the mother, is powerless to oversee. In fact, there were a sufficient number of young men who seemed to enjoy Margaret's society and came to the house and took her to parties, so I gave no special attention heed to this man almost twenty years Margaret's senior. However, it was he who made her feel that, at 20 years of age, she wanted to settle down to wifehood and leave the home of her childhood and girlhood.
>
> *Emma Bourne*

Margaret had many deliberate conversations with her mother during this time, saying, "Mother, Giles is right for me. He has many credentials. He obtained an engineering degree from a prestigious school. He's an accomplished sales person and businessman, and has plans to become a stock broker. Father should be pleased that he wants to be in a financial industry, one that can be considered very lucrative. He's kind and considerate of my needs, and he truly loves me."

Emma remained unconvinced. "Margaret, what happens when he decides to go off on one of his adventures you love to hear about? How can you be so sure he will return to you?"

Margaret responded, "If he goes on one of his adventures, I will go with him. I'm convinced he is the right choice."

Emma, still not persuaded, said, "Well, if you are sure. But your father will take some convincing."

Margaret pressed on, "Father will come around. Giles is a businessman like pops, and he will show father his worth. I'm sure of it."

Margaret usually got her way, no matter what the consequences. Edwin knew how to deal with boys, but became rather befuddled when it came to his daughter. He wanted to be strong, but just couldn't set rules for his daughter without them being overridden by Emma.

In May of 1922, they announced their engagement. Emma organized a Tea on May 15th for Margaret's friends and made the announcement.[13] As the engagement continued, Giles continued to be attentive throughout the summer as preparations were made for the wedding. He drove to New Bedford each weekend from Boston to get to know the family better and to help with wedding preparations. Emma seemed to warm up to him through his attentiveness and his interest in making the wedding a beautiful success and the reception a sociable event.[14]

Giles also busied himself in the Boston area. He found an apartment complex in Cambridge with a suite on the top floor. Margaret and Emma would travel to Cambridge to furnish the kitchen and the rest

---

[13] Emma Taber Bourne in her journal for Margaret describes the engagement in this way, "So, on May 15, Margaret's engagement to Giles Calkins was announced at a Tea we gave her at home for her Club girls and a few others."

[14] Emma Taber Bourne in her journal describes his involvement, "Giles in the meantime came down weekends for we wanted to see him and get acquainted with the new member of the family."

TO ENDURE – REKINDLED LOVE

of the house with appliances and furniture.[15]

Emma appreciated the Giles' qualities. His gentle nature showed through, and he genuinely cared how Margaret felt and attended to her needs. She could see how Margaret had become infatuated with him. These same qualities irked Edwin Senior. He expected Margaret's mate to be stern and commanding, neither of which described Giles. But, he and Emma both expected him to financially care for her; something that Giles felt he could do.

Emma continued to grow fond of Giles because of his attentive nature to Margaret. When Giles went skating with Margaret when they were courting, she fell and injured her pelvis[16]. Giles felt responsible for the incident. He would come to the hospital and read aloud. When he could not come, he would send flowers, candy, books and other gifts to remind her of his love.

Despite her father's concerns, Edwin agreed to the Church wedding in New Bedford, in part due to Emma's persuasion.

Margaret and Giles married each other on October 21, 1922, a clear, cool Saturday. After a long tedious summer of preparation, the well-attended wedding suited Emma. People came from all over New England and as far south as Florida

The First Unitarian Church of New Bedford

---

[15] Emma Taber Bourne in her journal describes the events, "In the meantime, Giles had been busy and had found a new apartment house in Cambridge and engaged a suite on the top floor becoming their new home. Margaret and I met up a few times and equipped the kitchenette etc. etc."

[16] Emma Taber Bourne in her journal describes the injury as "her back or rather the 'sacrum ilium' bone became misplaced."

and as far west as Chicago and even California. The ceremony commenced at the Unitarian Church, located on 8th street in New Bedford. The regal church sanctuary nicely accommodated the sizable wedding party. Edwin walked down the aisle with Margaret, with her hand in the crook of his arm, and gave away his daughter in front of his closest and dearest friends. He remained gracious during the wedding ceremony and gave Margaret a gentle kiss on the cheek as he gave her hand to Giles.

Emma described the wedding in her journal.

> Margaret's dress was white satin and was made at the same place where her "come out" dress was made. The bridesmaid's dresses were made there as well…. I wore a light gray, embossed velvet. Standish and Edwin *(Margaret's brothers)* were also ushers and of course they both looked very dear in my eyes.
>
> Exactly on the notch of 12:30 came the bridal procession. The good looking ushers followed by the bridesmaids in their deft colorings and the children with their flower baskets and then Margaret with her father. I must say right here that I hope someday she might witness as lovely a delight for herself—for she did look like a beautiful Queen as she stood there ready to meet her husband. She really looked worthy of the best of Earth's princes—for she looked a princess. The Church was exquisitely trimmed with palms and oak leaves and white chrysanthemums.
>
> *Emma Bourne's Journal*

The officiant provided a beautiful ceremony. He finally got to the point and asked the bride and groom to give their vows.

The bride began with her vows, starting with personal words and stating "I promise to love and cherish you all the days of my life. You are full of adventure and excitement. I want to be part that excitement." Then she gave the standard response: "I, Margaret, take thee, Giles, to be my

TO ENDURE – REKINDLED LOVE

wedded husband—to have and to hold from this day forward—for better or worse–for richer or poorer—in sickness and in health—to love and to cherish, till death do us part. According to God's holy ordinance—and there to, I give thee my troth."

Next, the groom gave his vows. "You are my princess and the love of my life. I will give my heart and soul to you and make you the happiest person on earth. My love for you will never diminish, and I will stay true to you for the rest of my life. I know God will be with us every day we are together." Then,: "I Giles, take thee, Margaret, to be my wedded wife—to have and to hold from this day forward—for better or worse—for richer or poorer—in sickness and in health—to love and to cherish, till death do us part. According to God's holy ordinance—and there to, I give thee my troth."

After the wedding, the happy couple exited to the Parish Hall where the reception commenced.

> The reception was held in the Parish. Hence, also beautifully decorated palms and oak leaves and white chrysanthemums. In the parlor we received our guests about 2:50. The wedding breakfast was ample and delicious. When finally all had been served, the bride had cut the cake at the table laid for the wedding party. She had stood on the stairs and threw the sprays from her bouquet to those most near and dear. Then changed her clothes for the going away gown. Our wedding drew to an end. The dear bride and groom left amid chimes of complete and many good wishes. Some of the guests were bidding us goodbye, saying what we heard since many times; that it was the prettiest wedding for many a long day and that was welcome to one said. For wasn't that what we had looked to have; a pretty wedding and a happy sociable reception.
>
> *Emma Bourne – Margaret's Journal*

Edwin and Emma received many complements on the result as guests were leaving.

While a happy occasion, Giles sensed tension in the air. Edwin had looked Giles directly in the eye before the ceremony and stated, "I am watching you. I fully expect you to do great things in this life and, above all, take excellent care of my daughter at all times. You will not disappoint me. Do you understand?"

Giles had no choice but to reply, "Yes, yes I do. Fully. You won't be disappointed." The unease only subsided at the end of the wedding, because now he could begin a life with his bride.

Giles worked hard to shake the dark distrust by the Bourne family that he engendered from the start. Although he did well in business selling securities when they married, he knew Edwin watched for any chink in his armor.

Chapter 3 – The Honeymoon

Margaret and Giles's honeymoon surprised everyone, because family expected Giles to take her on an expensive trip someplace exotic. Instead, he planned a honeymoon consisting of a camping and hunting trip in Maine.

Giles knew Margaret desperately wanted to get out of New Bedford, and he obliged her, but he wanted a unique adventure, one that he would enjoy as well. Giles knew of a nice hunting ground in Maine at Spencer Lakes. She had talked about her father's hunting trips, which intrigued Giles. He had arranged the honeymoon. He grabbed his gun and his camping equipment and jumped into his Cadillac. The Cadillac, fondly called "the old Caddy," reflected Giles's ambition. He packed it full of his camping gear to escape on the trip. Margaret packed a nice suitcase along with her best warm clothes. They left for their adventure.

On the road, Giles relaxed now that he was alone with Margaret and he could be himself. He became funny and chatty. She loved that about him. He knew so much. Being a proper New Bedford girl, she had not gone camping very often and had never been hunting. She had taken trips outside of New Bedford for short visits to relatives in Boston and

Larry Calkins

New York, but she never dreamt she would go to Maine for anything. She had briefly been to New Hampshire but never to Maine, and had heard about its natural beauty, and she wanted to see it.

On the long trip to Maine, Giles used the time to tell related or shortened stories of the west, about mining, and rounding up cattle as a cowboy. He knew she would be intrigued about mines in Colorado and Arizona where his father had a financial interest.

She would ask him, "Giles what type of mines were they?"

He responded, "Gold and silver mines. You know the silver set your parents have? Miners dug or blasted the raw silver from the rock, and then refined and purified the silver before it could be fashioned into a tea set like the ones in your parent's china cabinet that you adore."

Giles Calkins
My Father

"It takes a lot of work to refine silver so that it becomes pure." He did not want to bore her with too many details. "Suffice it to say, to manufacture silver requires much preparation and purification prior to the point the artist can fashion the silver pieces."

He visited some of mines and saw how the miners worked. They removed the gold and silver ore, separating it from the surrounding hard rock or from the gravel near the bedrock under a rerouted stream. Miners created huge slag piles of waste rock next to the screening and washing devices used. The gold dust found in some streams he described as tiny, but very valuable in larger quantities.

TO ENDURE – REKINDLED LOVE

Margaret said she wanted to see these mines. She openly daydreamed of striking it rich and all the things that she and Giles could buy with the gold and silver they would find. He warned her about the hard work required to extract the gold or silver and that the only ones who really made it rich included the owners of the mines and the merchants that sold mining supplies and provisions, exploiting the miners. He explained how his father had the right idea to partner with the owners through investing. She became enthralled. Despite the hardships, she wanted to see the mines even more.

Giles told her, "My father was a thrifty sort of person, but invested in almost everything, and he had a passion for mines."

He continued, "My father often invested in these mines sight unseen, sometimes even making money from these ventures." Giles knew that sometimes people claiming to be mine owners hoodwinked the investors and absconded with the investment money once they convinced the investors to invest. His father needed to be vigilant and skeptical. Giles stated his father only invested when he saw convincing evidence that he would turn a profit. He told Margaret of his father's astute business practices, hoping to further establish his own worth by association.

Through the boom and bust nature of the mining business, often he found the mines abandoned and his father's investments squandered or nonexistent. He tried to contact the owners, but rapidly found they were pretty close-mouthed about the mine. If pressed they claimed poverty or bankruptcy. He found one silver mine and some gold mines in Arizona still operating. When inquiring, he found that those mines were nearly finished, and the miners planned to leave the site for potential mining opportunities elsewhere. While he heard though the grapevine that the silver mine made hundreds of thousands of dollars, but he could not be sure of its success. He gathered a few nuggets of gold and bars of silver he found or purchased to describe his adventure. He tucked them away for safe keeping.

Giles told Margaret, "On my return trip I tried to think of a good way to explain what I found to my father and place it in the best light. I did not know what to tell him. I emphasized the working mines where the miners removed most of the silver." Giles continued, "I never really found out the full truth of any of my father's investments. Instead I found the gold rush influence and the tough, unforgiving life of a miner." It was a risky, cutthroat business.

He continued the explanation of his adventurous life stating that to get to the West, he needed to secure employment along the way. Since there weren't many opportunities for selling art or using his engineering skills, he needed to make ends meet as he traveled. He knew the approximate locations of the mines that his father had invested in, but he needed to cross vast landscapes to get to them, especially those in remote locations. When he ran out of money, he worked as a ranch-hand and cowboy. He would stop at a ranch along the way and ask for work, willing to do anything to make a few bucks to get to the next town.

Often he landed in an area weeks at a time, so it seemed like it took forever to travel from one location to another. Being young with a firm goal, he had all the time in the world. Bred a city boy, Giles knew little to nothing about being a cowboy, yet these ranching jobs were the most plentiful. Unfortunately, he admitted, the cowpokes called him a "green horn." He had compassionate bosses, but they also expected much

TO ENDURE – REKINDLED LOVE

from him. He woke up at dawn, rousted out of his sleeping bag on the ground by the foreman, and sent on his way to herd the cows from one pasture to another after a quick breakfast of coffee and bread. The trek often took most of the day and exhaustion overcame him come nightfall. The foreman would sometimes offer him some beans and bread as an evening meal and then he'd get some shuteye. The next morning, he did that all over again.

Giles also recounted stories of his father's other business ventures. Travis G. Calkins, his father, and Giles's uncles made a living manufacturing and selling barbed wire.

They discovered that cattle ranchers used miles of barbed wire to keep their cows within the boundaries of their multi-square mile ranches. Barbed wire also effectively deterred an enemy from advancing in periods of war.

When they first started, the Calkins brothers and their partners tried to start a business relationship with a gentleman named Joseph Glidden, who had held a patent, issued in 1874, for the manufacture of barbed wire. He and others inspired the Calkins brothers to get involved in the business.

> One who has tried, in the country, to get through a fence with only four or five wires to tear his clothing and otherwise punish him, will readily understand its effectiveness as a defense for war purposes. Barbed wire, set only a few inches apart and ten to twelve feet in height, surrounding forts and fortified positions in fifty or a hundred successive lines, can keep the enemy from advancing into critical areas.
>
> *Travis G. Calkins,*
> *my paternal Grandfather*

Larry Calkins

Glidden tried and failed to find the owner of an earlier patent called the Kelly patent. Initially, the Calkins brothers thought they would find Michael Kelly, the owner, and purchase the patent and offer to resell the patent to Glidden. The Kelly patent, issued in 1868 before the Glidden patent, held particular interest because it contained some features

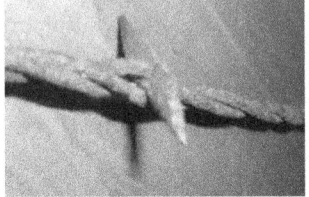

The Kelly Barbed Wire

Glidden may like. Through much effort, William Calkins, one of Giles' older brothers, found Michael Kelly in New York.

As William discussed arrangements with Mr. Kelly, Mr. Kelly described the origin of the idea as a boy when hedge fences broke down in Ireland. As a young man he wondered how to repair those fences. He first placed a piece of tin on a wire. Through revisions of his design, he came up with a double strand wire construction with one strand containing a sharp, triangular barb pierced through the center spaced at regular intervals along the wire, and the second strand of wire holding the barb in place.

William negotiated with Mr. Kelly, and Kelly agreed to sell the patent to the Calkins brothers because Mr. Kelly had not used, nor had he any plans for his patent. When William Calkins returned to Chicago, he found Glidden, and his partner, had made a success out of Glidden's patent by beginning the manufacturing and sale of their product. The Calkins brothers decided not to offer the Kelly patent to Glidden. Instead, they began their own manufacturing business using the patent from Kelly. Founded in 1878, the Calkins brothers called their company the Kelly Barbed Wire Company. The brothers then hired a mechanic to design a machine to make the Kelly wire. They established the manufacturing process and began manufacturing and selling their own product. Travis G. successfully sold the manufactured product to ranchers and farmers from Chicago eastward.

A few years later, a competitor, the Washburn, Moen Company of Worcester, Massachusetts, produced simply a plain wire, which could not compete with other barbed wire manufacturers. Washburn began looking for opportunities. Late in 1888, they first approached Glidden and his partner, who would not sell. Washburn then sent attorneys to the Kelly Company. In May 1889, Washburn offered to pay the Calkins brothers a royalty of seventy-five cents per hundred pounds on all the barbed wire made by them until the Kelly patent expired. The first half year's royalties amounted to over $37,000. In the ninth and last year, 1889, royalties amounted $150,000.[17]

Giles, my eventual father, was pleased when Margaret was impressed by his father and uncles. Even in the 1920's, $37,000 to $150,000 per year remained a good amount of money and provided a solid basis for future investments.

Then, Giles became sentimental.

Giles began, "My mother is now a widow and will need much of the money father invested. I worry about her. She is still managing to stay in their home in Evanston Illinois, but she relied on him and now he is gone. I hope she uses that investment. She is thrifty, but that money will go quickly if there is a downturn in the economy or she has medical

---

[17] The Story of Barbed Wire – By Travis G. Calkins, 1878, Ashland Ave, Evanston, Illinois

bills."

Margaret listened to Giles silently. She expressed her thoughts about him "as a person who could do almost anything."

During his travels, Giles found places like the Grand Canyon. To aid him with his artwork, Giles would often use his prized Kodak Brownie 2 camera to take pictures of his subjects and, then when he time allowed, would create an etching from those photographs capturing the detail of the massive canyon and its interesting features. He also created etchings of pueblos where native people lived, as well as watercolor painting of native peoples entering their adobe homes. The interesting structures and raw beauty he saw pleased him, and he packed his art supplies despite how awkward they were to bring on such a journey.

Etching
The Grand Canyon
by Giles Calkins

Margaret enjoyed Giles's stories greatly.

***

Even though they left early that morning, it took most of the day to travel there. Giles's stories helped pass the time as they drove together on the long road to Maine. The town they were headed toward, if you can call it that, was called "The Forks" or "The Forks Plantation," with a population of thirty-five, including twelve households. Giles had driven the route several times before and found the roads very passible for this time of the year. When they arrived at The Forks, they took the main

TO ENDURE – REKINDLED LOVE

road to the northwest and drove out of town.

After that, the road narrowed and Giles's stories got shorter and periodically interrupted as they approached the site. Giles drove down a dusty road with potholes galore for the last 10 miles. Even in the Old Caddy, the potholes jarred bones. The bumpy roads made talking difficult, but didn't hinder the anticipation as they neared their destination.

***

Margaret persevered. Finally, Giles took a hard left though a gap in the fence line, driving through the open forested area. The only way to follow the path was to watch for the gap in the trees or catch a glimpse of tire tracks beneath the grass, died leaves or pine needles. The Maine landscape was beautiful, making the trip worthwhile with large gorgeous trees on either side of the roadway. She was somewhat conflicted, but Margaret continued to wait for the adventure to begin. They crossed a small stream and climbed to the top of a small rise.

They'd finally arrived. Giles pulled up to a rustic cabin that would provide them a roof overhead. Margaret noted the overcast sky, the leaves turning yellowish green with hints of red, some of which had already fallen, and the crisp autumn air. Dusk came early in the Maine autumn forests and the sky became darker. Giles fired up his lantern. Both of them could hardly wait to get unpacked to begin their time together. Giles gathered his hunting gear, cooking utensils and bedroll. Margaret grabbed her suitcase.

They stayed at a cabin called "Hiawatha Cabin." Inside the cabin, the wooden bed with a mattress seemed dusty and smelled of mildew. It would do, but, again, Margaret imagined things a little different. She saw a sink, but without running water. It became obvious that the small and large bucket nearby the sink meant something. Margaret quickly discovered that the only water came from the stream running to the lake several hundred feet away from the cabin. She also realized she needed to use an outhouse located in the opposite direction of the stream. She remained determined to make the best of this situation. They retired for the evening exhausted, but happy to be together, still managing to do what newlyweds do. Both finally fell asleep around midnight.

Margaret awoke before morning light, but fell back to sleep and slept in until about 9AM. When she woke, she made herself and Giles some breakfast and decided to take a look around. They took a walk and discovered a nearby cabin, which they later learned served as a local bar, and was known as the "clubhouse." Both of them laughed at the thought of unlimited booze coming from little cabin. They spent the rest of the day sitting by the lake, relaxing at the cabin, and going to the clubhouse.

After a couple of days into a relaxing honeymoon, Margaret became a little worried that Giles forgot about his bride because he busied himself with preparing for the hunting trip the following day, but he kept reassuring her that he loved the outdoors, and hoped that this trip would be a way for him to share that love with her. It was obvious that he was self-reliant, because he made preparations for both of them by unpacking and getting their guns ready to hunt. The countryside teamed with deer, and she knew he would easily be able to bag that deer he dreamed of soon. That evening, Giles and Margaret met the guide at their cabin.

TO ENDURE – REKINDLED LOVE

Herbie Durgin, who knew these woods like the back of his hand, explained the hunt would take place early the next morning. Both Giles and Margaret needed to wake by 5AM and be ready to go. Herbie had scouted for the deer herds already and found where the deer bedded down. He knew exactly where to take Giles and his bride.

Margaret listened intently to Herbie talk and it reminded her of her father's stories of hunting trips to New Hampshire and Maine. She remembered when Edwin had brought back moose meat and deer meat with much fanfare. Now, she had the opportunity to experience the pleasure of hunting firsthand with Giles.

As planned, they woke early the next morning. Herbie greeted them outside their cabin. As he pointed north, he explained, "We are going along the lake on a trail, then over a ridge and into a valley. Don't worry about a thing. You'll be back before you know it."

They hiked along Spencer Lake on a trail fittingly called the "Enchanted Trail." The trail wound through beautiful forest with its foliage turning colors. Yes, Margaret saw its enchantment.

Margaret commented to Giles, "Look at the lake; it's so serene and beautiful. You can see for miles. I feel like I inherited this vast kingdom with no one around. Maybe, kings and queens will show up any minute or at least a knight in shining armor, because I feel like a princess."

Giles responded, "You are a princess."

"And you are my Knight in Shining Armor," Margaret added

They continued to hike for what seemed like hours and found the perfect place along Spencer Lake for a permanent camp. They quickly set up camp and hiked for another half mile to a place called Birchwood Point, where they slowed down and became quiet.

Herbie pointed down into a draw where they saw a small herd of deer. It included a buck and three does. They circled around and crouched down in the woods to wait for the deer to get into position. Margaret had one doe in her gun sights. Giles leveled his rifle on the buck and prepared to shoot. Herbie told them to wait. They did as the deer inched closer. Herbie motioned to Margaret to shoot, one finger pointed at her, then moving his hand toward the doe. The doe got within 100 yards of Margaret, and she pulled the rifle's trigger; the shot reverberated. The buck looked up, startled, and Giles took aim and shot the buck in the heart; a clean shot. A third shot rang out from Herbie's gun, and the doe staggered and fell to the ground. Herbie planned to be the backup in case one of the shots missed or only wounded the animal. Herbie had shot the doe because Margaret's shot went over the deer, missing it completely. Giles and Margaret stood in disbelief until Herbie motioned for both of them to go to the animals.

They bagged not only one deer, but two. She watched as Giles and Herbie took their knives and began to clean the carcasses so just the meat and hide remained. Margaret went to the local stream to get some water to help clean the animals. It took them a long time, but finally got to the point where Giles and Herbie felt they could pack the carcasses back to the camp they had set up along the lake. They struggled with both animals. The buck weighed 133 pounds and had antlers with six points; not a large animal but still reasonably sized. Some of the trophy bucks weigh over 200 pounds. The doe weighed 105 pounds, and was a

TO ENDURE – REKINDLED LOVE

healthy animal in her own right but still smaller than many of the does in the area. At the camp, they cut a few steaks off of the buck to have for a midday dinner. Margaret, again, grabbed the bucket, and went to the stream to gather water to help wash off the knife and help clean the carcass. They worked as a team under Herbie's supervision. Margaret felt Giles appreciated her help.

While Giles started a fire for dinner, Margaret gathered cooking utensils and frying pan with a long wooden handle. She placed the steaks he cut into the pan and began cooking. Margaret noticed him reaching for his sketchpad beginning to draw. She went back to cooking and appeared oblivious to the drawing, just happy to be with Giles, and happy to finally be doing something useful. Margaret took her time, and not many words were exchanged. The venison stakes, mostly cooked through,

Drawing "Margaret on Honeymoon" by Giles Calkins

were eaten and enjoyed. Herbie bid them goodbye, stating he would be back to help bring the deer to the cabin in the late-morning. Margaret and Giles both agreed. Through the cold night, they bundled up together, wondering what adventures lay ahead tomorrow.

The next morning, Margaret woke first in the crisp air. The birds sang and a slight breeze whispered through the trees that rustled the leaves. The fall air smelled fresh, but felt brisk. She got up and started cooking the eggs and toast they packed for the occasion. The morning began peaceful and serine with the stream babbling nearby. All her senses were heightened because of the surrounding beauty and the relevance of that moment and none of her surroundings were taken for granted. When Giles awoke, he rose to the smell of eggs cooking, the fire crackling, and birds singing.

He told her, "I'm genuinely impressed with your ability to start a fire by yourself."

She replied, "I saw an ember still burning from last night and found some kindling to add. It started right up. Then, I added a few larger pieces of wood." She laughed, "I'm a genius."

Later that day, Giles and Herbie hoisted the deer carcasses onto their pack boards and hiked back to the cabin with the animals dragging behind. The men finished dressing the animals by hanging them upside down from the eaves of the cabin. The animals would need to be kept covered during the day to prevent the flies from attacking them. At night, the air was cool, almost refrigerator-like, to preserve them.

The following day, the newlyweds left, Herbie and Giles placed the doe and buck onto the running board of the Caddy.

Giles said, "Herbie I want to thank you very much for your help these last few days. We couldn't have found those deer and had such a successful trip without you."

Margaret chimed in, "Yes, Herbie, thank you. We had a delightful time and you helped make that time the best."

Herbie replied with a tip of his hat toward Margaret and a handshake with Giles.

The venison traveled home on the running boards for the 300

TO ENDURE – REKINDLED LOVE

mile trip back to Cambridge and their new apartment. The venison had a rented cold-storage unit waiting for it. The Caddy, loaded with the carcasses and the gear they came with, added to the complexity of the trip home. Giles and Margaret were happy to have the Caddy work well enough to bring themselves and their cargo safely home. Giles described the journey home, it was "the end of a Perfect Honeymoon." Margaret wasn't so sure.

Larry Calkins

TO ENDURE – REKINDLED LOVE

Chapter 4 – My birth

My parents lived in their new apartment on Linnaean Street in Cambridge, Massachusetts. Just prior to my birth in August 1923, Margaret had a visit from Katherine Squires, known as Casey, a long-time childhood friend and roommate from Lincoln School. She remained unmarried, living with her mother in Evanston, Illinois where she cooked and cared for her. Casey taught kindergarten that allowed her time to care for her mother and have summers off. For the most part, her mother could cook and care for herself as long as she had periodic help from a friend or neighbor. Consequently, Casey did not think twice about traveling out east to see Margaret, keep her company and be a good diversion. She spent some time with Margaret until my birth.

Upon arrival, Margaret picked up Casey at the train station in Boston. In the Caddy on their way back to Cambridge, Casey threw her arms around Margaret as she is driving giving her a bigger than life hug and in her best high voice, sounding somewhat like a kindergartener she taught, said, "Kitty, I missed you so much." Margaret needed to admonish Casey, explaining how dangerous grabbing her while driving was. Still, Casey had a helpful and chatty nature, filling Margaret's days with joyful ways and happy antics stating she could stay to help until her classes restarted in September.

Mother liked her very much, but also continued to be cautious of her at the same time knowing that Casey tended to be innocent and spontaneous in mannerism and her actions sometimes put her in a dangerous or uncomfortable situation. Casey's visit coincided with Mother being eight months pregnant with me, so Casey helped and became a confident for Margaret during that last month.

Just before my birth, Mother and Dad rented a large, two-story home on George Street in Newton. Casey helped with the move. Dad wanted my first home to be comfortable for the whole family. Margaret responded to Casey, "I'm so happy you came and were able to help me though this last month of pregnancy. I couldn't have done it without you."

Casey stayed, leaving right after my birth. Giles uncharitably commented to a close friend and client, "And Casey stayed and stayed."

My birth on September 9, 1923, in Newton, Massachusetts, made my mother elated and Dad very proud. He gave me the name: Travis. Instead of using the name Giles for me, Dad decided I should be called "Travis," in memory of his father.

A year passed with my new parents learning how to care for me. It included visits from Grandparents and friends and other relatives. Then, just prior to Christmas 1924, my father came home to share his good fortune with Mother and me. My father had purchased our first home; a nice Christmas present for the family. This smaller two-story home in nearby Newtonville, Massachusetts, became the location of my

TO ENDURE – REKINDLED LOVE

second Christmas.

We lived on Central Avenue in Newtonville, a block away from Lowell Park and about a half mile from the Charles River. The house suited the needs of our young family nicely. The home had a large front porch surrounded by a cris-crossed railing between a top and bottom rail. Pillars reached to the roof with a decorative joist holding up the ceiling of the porch. The bay window from the living room looked out onto the front yard. It made a nice place for a photograph.

My father sold commodities and a few stocks after Mother and he were married. They settled in Newton and in the 1920s, and he did very well for himself. He loved going downtown to Boston to his office, talking to his clients, and discussing his adventures and perspective on life. He enjoyed talking to people more than he liked selling commodities. He felt at home selling metals, like pig iron, because at Yale he became a metallurgical engineer. Selling metals also reconnected him with his deceased father and his father's barbed wire enterprise, except he just sold the raw product. He was well acquainted with the process of making steel, which made the raw pig iron easy to sell to steel manufacturers. He could talk processes with the buyers and understood their frustrations and needs in quality products.

My father's interest in metals grew because he loved to etch portraits or pictures on copper plates and make prints out of the drawings. He also had a connection with his father through being a stockbroker. That type of work came easily for him. He remembered every shred of advice his father gave him and freely offered similar advice to his clients, creating a successful business to provide for his family. It helped that, during the 1920s the stock market did quite well.

Larry Calkins

My parents maintained a comfortable lifestyle; not bad for a new family starting out.

My mother busied herself with taking care of me and keeping the home in an orderly fashion. My mother, tired most of the time, still attempted to keep things in ship shape condition. She had help from her mother Emma, receiving advice and counsel from her on everything from shopping, to caring for me, from house maintenance, to the normal frustrations between married couples.

As a respite on the weekends, Dad took his family to Nonquitt, Massachusetts. Mother's family owned a cottage at Nonquitt on the coast of southeastern Massachusetts. The family enjoyed the getaway on the weekends. Sometimes we would spend the weekend. I had fond memories of the Nonquitt cottage. Sometimes the Bourne's would show up at the cottage as well, including Mother's brothers' family. Rarely, but on occasion their showing up created a strain between the adults, but the kids always enjoyed each other's company.

****

My father traded in the old Caddy, and purchased a new car, a Packard, that provided good transportation for our family.

During the fall of 1924, Mother, Dad and I drove to New Haven Connecticut and too see the Yale vs. Army football game. We stopped to stay the night at Great Barrington, Massachusetts, at an old Mansion, on the way. We froze that evening at the mansion. Any heat in the place dissipated as soon as it reached the room. We could feel the frigid breeze outside, flowing through the walls and permeating our very being. You couldn't put enough blankets on the bed to keep us warm enough.

TO ENDURE – REKINDLED LOVE

My father loved talking about Yale and was excited to attend the game. He could hardly wait to get to New Haven. His excitement soared when he saw the old familiar buildings. He anticipated meeting his old classmates, and of course watching Yale beat Army.

My father predicted great things for the game as he related the previous season to my mother. "Last year, Yale had an undefeated season with eight wins, no ties and no losses. Thomas Albert Dwight Jones—everyone calls him TAD for short—is the coach for the Yale Bulldogs. TAD was the Bulldog quarterback in 1906 and 1907 and became quite a football hero. Back then, the team beat Harvard, their rival."

The fact that TAD played football for Yale with such a great record wasn't lost on her. She asked, "So, when did TAD start coaching at Yale."

My father responded, "He returned to coach the Bulldogs in 1920. Last year, TAD coached the undefeated season, and this year it looks very promising too. So far, the team has beat North Carolina, Georgia, and Brown Universities. They also played Dartmouth, but tied them at 14-14. I think they will take Army to the cleaners."

When they arrived, they found the stadium. My mother marveled at the largest stadium in the US called the "Yale Bowl", seating 70,896 people and completed just a few years earlier in 1914.[18]

The Yale vs. Army game started. The excitement of the crowd

---

[18] The stadium inspired the construction of the current day Rose Bowl and the Super Bowl. Its façade design echoed the Yale campus' neo-Gothic design.

built around them as the players ran up and down the field. Dad caught the excitement of the game. Mother, too, enjoyed the excitement and most importantly Dad's company, but also had her hands full caring for me. My father pointed out key plays and tried to explain the game to her, helping assure her understanding of actions on the field. She had attended high school football games, watching her brother, Richard, play, but she herself had attended an all-girls school and appreciated further explanation about the game. Between Richard previously talking about how to play football, and my father's current explanations, she felt involved in the game.

At one point, a huge roar enveloped the other side of the stadium. It woke me from my slumber. My father observed, "Damn, Army just scored." Six points went up on the score board, then seven.

As the game continued, I fell back to sleep. Later, I again awoke with a start. The whole stadium erupted in a huge roar of excitement. I started to cry as if I asked "what happened?"

My father's reassuring voice calmed me with, "We just made a touchdown, little guy."

The game continued on, with both teams battling back and forth, until the final countdown. The game finally finished. Army had seven points and Yale had seven points. The hopes of beating Army had vanquished, but the satisfaction of remaining undefeated another season remained.

Yale finished the season with six wins, two ties and no losses.

***

TO ENDURE – REKINDLED LOVE

My father often reflected on his life. He dearly loved me and my mother. In 1923 and 1924, we took numerous mini-vacations relaxing on the weekend in Nonquitt, in the woods, or on the beach. It became obvious to Mother how much he adored being a father. Mother would take underexposed pictures of us together, either Dad sitting near me or holding me in his arms. At times, he looked at me as if he couldn't believe his fortune. Mother said he marveled at every word I said, or step I took.

Dad and me

Similar pictures were taken of the dogs my mother adored. Mother tended carefully to her dogs: Mugs, Peter Chinook, and Peggy, the Airedale Terriers. Pictures of each of these dogs with my mother created fond memories for my parents.

Every once in a while, my mother would steal the camera, and in the most sweet or sometimes awkward moment of my father, she would snap a shot. My father labeled one snapshot of himself and me as "Ikey and Travis." Presumably "Ikey" was a nickname I gave him that he owned and it stuck.

Every once in a while, Dad would reflect on his life and how he offended my mother in some way. He could not bear to upset her. My mother grabbed the camera one day while they were in a nearby forest, laughing at his demise and playfully snapped a picture to bring my father out of his funk.

Giles Calkins "Nit Wit"

Larry Calkins

He responded as he always did to her, smiling and returning to his old self. He laughed at the thought and titled a picture of himself, "Nit Wit."

TO ENDURE – REKINDLED LOVE

Chapter 5 – My Sister

In addition to my parents, my grandmother, Emma, adored me too, and when my sister came along, she thought our family was the perfect family. Mother gave birth to Sarah, my sister, on January 3, 1926, at the Newton Hospital—the same place she gave birth to me over two years earlier. Sarah completed our family. Her full name was Sarah Howland Calkins, a nod to my great grandmother, Sarah Jane Howland. The original Howland family name, Sarah's relatives, were prominent business people of the 19th century in New Bedford and often the Howland name was used for our relatives as a way to pass along that family name. My father fondly called her "Sady (pronounced Sa de)." Both my maternal grandparents started paying attention to Sarah, and I felt a little left out[19].

Dad, and Sarah In Waban

Just after Sarah's birth, Father and Mother decided a larger

---

[19] Later in life, I would grow to cherish our relationship and write her letters that expressed my deepest secrets and frustrations. Her positive influence on me brightened my day. As children, we played quite well together throughout our young lives.

house in Waban, a section of Newton and a suburb of Boston, would better meet the needs of their growing family. We spent Sarah's first Christmas in our new home in Waban.

Our new family home, located on Avalon Road in Waban, seemed friendlier and more accommodating than the previous Newton house. The Dutch Colonial, two-story house, a nice-looking home[20], commanded respect and reflected the affluence of its owner. Its location allowed my father to remain within reasonable commuting distance of downtown Boston where he did most of his business.

Margaret and Giles Calkins
My Mother and Father

Garbo, our German Shepard-mix dog, fiercely protected our family. I do not ever remember a time without a dog as part of our family. Dad and Mother took a great many pictures of our dogs showing their love of animals. Our cohesive family unit, including the dogs, provided a very loving environment to grow up in.

---

[20] I visited it sixty years later, and the house looks like it always did with a half-acre lot. The large lot, undoubtedly, still hides Mother's diamond engagement ring. Presumably, I threw it from an upstairs window. Nobody knows for sure, but my parents always assumed me to be the culprit. I have lived with this guilt all these years. For some reason the maid, or serviceman or a guest were never mentioned as possible suspects. Sarah may even have swallowed it. She may be worth much more than she knows, but I never heard these theories advanced. In reality, I hope someone found it and is richer for finding it. It would be a shame if it went down the toilet.

TO ENDURE – REKINDLED LOVE

Mother took her position in life seriously and took on her role with gusto. With two children, Mother had her hands full. As a playful two-year-old when Sarah's birth occurred, Garbo and I were pals. We played together, we walked, ran and hiked together and we got in trouble together. Mother tried hard keeping up with me and Garbo while also caring for a newborn baby. Mother ended each week totally exhausted while my father worked away from the home during the weekdays. Dad loved us dearly, but he found it difficult to come home and have two young children stretch his abilities.

As soon as my father would walk through the door after a busy day at work, my mother would toss him an exasperated and worn out look, pleading for help. Dad obliged the best he could, but his talents lay elsewhere. If his assignment required him to change a diaper or to dole out discipline, he again called on Mother.

During our youth, Dad found other interests like spending more time at his men's club or at a friend's house, rather than come home and face Mother and us children. To remedy the situation, Mother would periodically to go to her parents' house sixty-two miles away for the weekend or even a whole week where her mother helped take care of us. Occasionally, my grandmother, who did not drive, provided substantial help and came to Waban. I assume Mother went to pick her up. My grandmother set a framework for Mother, who appreciated the structure, as well as helping with dinner preparation and caring for us. Later, especially toward 1928 and 1929, nurse Winifred cared for us during the day and helped Mother with the cooking. That would free Mother up to do the things she wanted like knitting and putting on tea's for other ladies in the neighborhood.

Larry Calkins

Mother often wondered out loud how other families managed with many more children, since six to eight children were commonplace. One boy and one girl seemed to be enough.

***

Dad loved to drive his Packard. In the 1920s it seemed we always were going somewhere. We spent summers in Nonquitt at the Bourne family cabin. We also took trips to Cape Cod for a mini-vacation.

In 1926, we drove to New Haven, Connecticut for my father's 20-year reunion. My father tremendously enjoyed the reunion, reconnecting with old friends, reminiscing about the past, and catching up on the in-between years. He filled in the blanks, but, most importantly, he wanted to show off his new family and tell everyone about his happy life.

Being a little older now, I enjoyed running and playing outside on the Yale campus. I ran from one building to another, playing hide and seek with Mother as I ran between the bushes lining the walkways. Mother made things appear easy and she wanted the other women to think that she could raise children and entertain as well, without worry. It appeared to be a snap for her, but she really worked at the appearance. She was able to charm the other ladies showing that she could watch the children and simultaneously carrying on a meaningful conversation. She may have stretched the truth a bit.

Mother offered, "When Giles heads to Boston to meet with his clients, I take Travis to pre-school, and then I can focus on Sarah. Sometimes I have a tea for other mothers in the neighborhood when I am able to put Sarah down for a nap." She expressed herself well and made things sound very good indeed despite the truth about the daily struggle and the help she received from her mother.

***

In 1927, we spent a summer at Bay View on Cape Cod; it was a very enjoyable time for the whole family. We kids were full of spirit and our small family enjoyed each other most of the time. Our parents tried to relax, but I kept them busy as I ran around, played games and frolicked in the water. Sarah wanted to keep up with me, but she had just begun to walk, so she became no match for me. We created many fond memories on the Cape.

***

Later that year for Christmas, we drove to New York to Dad's sister's home, Lucile and Ernie Moncrieff's. Ernie worked in the oil business and made a good living from buying and selling oil stocks on Wall Street. Lucile and her family enjoyed a comfortable lifestyle and had a large home in New York.

During that trip, while the adults were in a middle of a discussion, my older cousin, whose name was also Lucille, but spelled with three l's, and I slipped away so she could show me her bike. I begged her to ride it. Unfortunately, she let me. I went careening down her steep driveway, hit a patch of ice at the bottom, and went head over heels into a car windshield breaking it into pieces. The plate glass used for windows in the vehicles, when it broke, broke into large, jagged pieces.[21] I cut my arm and face badly on the glass. Mother found me first and yelled, "Giles come quick. Travis's been in a bad accident."

My father rushed down the hill toward me. He gathered me up off the pavement, gently placed me in the rear seat of the Packard and rushed me to the local emergency room where I received several dozen stitches. My left arm didn't regain feeling in places from the scars and my face was also scarred. Such is the way of kids.

When I returned to the Moncrieff's, Mother said, "Next time Travis, I assume you won't be as anxious to be such a daredevil. You're such a boy."

She meant it more as a compliment than a reprimand, but it came across as being stern. Dad exhausted, just expressed relief. I had my adventure; the result scarred me; but I would live and see another day.

***

Dad sometimes spent weekday evenings home alone when Mother took Sarah and me to New Bedford and then would catch up with us on the weekends. Mother either brought us back to Waban for the weekend, or Dad might travel to New Bedford or Nonquitt. My mother remained dedicated to her husband and family and fully expected to see her marriage through. Any visit to see her mother became strictly a temporary situation to help her recharge her senses. Dad also understood the need and relented in a sympathetic way. Her childhood home, where she felt comfortable, rejuvenated her soul and spirit. There was little time

---

[21] It's not like today where safety glass is used in car windows that breaks into a million small pieces to prevent major injury.

TO ENDURE – REKINDLED LOVE

to do the artwork that he cherished, or to go to the men's club or other friends' houses. He settled on the routine of traveling back and forth when Mother took us to New Bedford, and she appreciated his flexibility.

That's why Dad cherished the vacations to the Cape and other places. He could afford it, and he made it part of his life. Everyone looked forward to those retreats.

Larry Calkins

TO ENDURE – REKINDLED LOVE

Chapter 6 – Growing Up in the late 1920s

Sarah and I were raised and cared for primarily by our mother, Nurse Winifred, or with the help of Grandmother often during the week. My father's care came mostly on the weekends that I loved. Dad chatted with me and my sister about how the week went. He articulated details about his clients and their families, never using their names. I explained the adventures Sarah and I had together. He showed us his paintings and etchings and talked about his adventures in the west. He captivated my sister, Sarah and me, when we saw his artwork and heard stories how he created his etchings. We listened intently as we took long walks with him and learned about many exciting things from his previous life.

I really liked his mining stories and fantasized about finding the hidden treasures. It seemed more like a treasure hunt rather than actual mining. As Dad would tell it, he traveled through the landscape seeing the Grand Canyon, the Rocky Mountains and the Great Plains. He told us how he trekked through the west traveling by train, by horse and sometimes by car, but mostly by foot. Part of the fun resulted from traveling to the mines. Sarah and I

Sarah and me

hunted for make-believe treasures in the back yard, digging them up and burying them again.

Sarah asked me, "Travis, are we going to dig for treasure today?"

I smiled, "Yes, that's a great idea." We finished what we were doing and raced to get our coats on to go outside.

Once outside, I'd exclaim, "There's the Grand Canyon. Let's go visit it. Maybe there is some treasure down there."

We would explore for hours. Dad would come outside and ask, "Find any treasure yet?"

I'd respond, "Oh yes, look at the gold nuggets I found," while bringing him common pebbles from the backyard.

He would chuckle and comment, "That's quite a nugget, Travis. It must be worth hundreds, if not thousands, of dollars."

I agreed and went to find more treasures.

Sometimes Dad would laugh and ask if we were "digging to China." Mother also liked the fact that we played so well together, imitating our father and his adventures.

I started school in Waban, attending kindergarten, and then first grade. I walked to school.[22]

---

[22] Much to my surprise upon return to the scene some sixty years later, I rediscovered the distance from our house to the school was a good long way -- at least a half mile. Schools provided buses for trips like that now days.

TO ENDURE – REKINDLED LOVE

In first grade, I took a nugget of gold and some raw silver in rock form to school for show and tell. I explained the adventures of my father. I told them about the gold mines and the silver mines and how my father investigated his father's investments, how he found the miners digging the gold and silver treasures from the ground. As I related the stories I knew so well, I mimicked Sarah and my adventures in our backyard, digging in our imagined mines. The kids ate up the stories, and they oohed and awed at the gold and silver I brought to class.

When we went to New Bedford and stayed with our grandparents, mother and grandmother, Emma, took good care of us during the day and allow Sarah and me to have our adventures while they did the housework or chatted. While during the day they kept a watchful eye on us, the delight during the day faded into the evenings. But the weekday evenings were not as fun. My grandfather, Edwin, often watched us after dinner, and he would peer above his newspaper glaring at me playing in front of him. If I left the room, he barked at me to get back where he could see me. I hated him. I did not feel I could do anything right. He rarely left me alone or said a kind word to me.[23]

***

Things never were quite right between my father and his in-laws since Mother and he married. The Bourne's, particularly the elder Edwin, doubted that the Calkins marriage would last.

---

[23] He must have been afraid I would grow up and be like my father. I don't remember my cousins experiencing similar attitudes by him. It seemed he charmed everyone else and made a good living in his day.

Larry Calkins

Grandfather tried to be cordial with my father, but held strong opinions. Still, my father tried to please Grandfather earning a good salary for his fledgling family. Dad felt he and his father-in-law had the financial industry in common and wanted to improve their relationship. He listened to Grandfather to glean wisdom to make him a better stockbroker. My father looked past Grandfather's condescending tone and searched for pearls of wisdom. Dad tried to curry favor with Grandfather.

My father felt being a stockbroker used science more than art. He used certain principles to choose stocks and securities and felt he had experience to make good judgements. For the most part, he did make good judgements. He respected Grandfather's position in New Bedford and felt the elder had raised a good family. Dad loved Grandfather's daughter very much, but ultimately, any ingratiation Dad tried failed because whatever Dad suggested Grandfather differed.

Being a former banker, Grandfather knew about the financial world, had good friends who were stockbrokers, and enjoyed a measure of respect in New Bedford. Grandfather's approach focused on investing in local New Bedford stocks. He knew the companies, and had good relationships with the textile industry because he had loaned money to them. He expected the New Bedford businesses to keep him afloat as long as he kept investing. He did not see why steel mills or other national companies that his son-in-law suggested would be a better investment than New Bedford stocks. Even Joe, his son, recognized his father made a mistake by only investing in local stocks alone. Grandfather may also have been bitter because he retired from the banking business and his lifestyle had downsized since his children were grown. Is it possible that

TO ENDURE – REKINDLED LOVE

Grandfather was bitter about being replaced as President with his protégé, William Cook, by Uncle Fred? As a representative, Grandfather still had a responsibility to uphold the Taber—Bourne family reputation. He shouldered the heavy social and financial burden of the family. Now, Grandfather solely relied on his investments. My father was an easy target for Grandfather's frustration. His biting tone was designed to show my father that they had a different approach to business, and Grandfather had more experience and was wiser.

Grandfather would say, "Stop the niceties with your clients. It's not doing you any good. Explain the rules, give them your advice and go on to the next client. You need to be strict in how you approach the client, making sure you get the proper commission."

My father handled the approach to business differently, "If you don't express interest in their lives, you don't find out how best to help your clients. You may be giving them lousy advice."

Grandfather pressed, "You have my daughter and her family to support. You've got to draw lines."

My father tried to help his clients in a symbiotic relationship where they made money and he received a fee, either in the form of a percentage or a straight fee for service. Due to his Christian upbringing, Dad felt an honest, kind and straightforward approach worked well and he did not need to resort to other tactics to earn a decent living. Still, too often, the two men got together, arguments over business practices arose.

Mother loved both her husband and her father and did not like the disagreements. She also liked the finer things in life. Her fun loving, self-assured outlook on life allowed her to be outgoing, outspoken, and well versed about most any topic. Her demeanor and beauty also empowered her to hold her head high and present herself in a confident way.

Being in the banking business, my grandfather knew he needed to be cordial with his customers, but the banking business had rules. Folks needed to follow the rules and could not deviate. The rules helped New England patrons feel they could trust the banking institution. Trust remained all important. Chatting with one customer would take away from working with another customer. The other customers would be standing in line, and he could not afford to waste time with idle chit-chat. He expected my father to handle his business the same. Volume in the banking business remained the most important.

Grandfather felt that if my father chatted with one customer, he could not attract other customers. He needed to be disciplined. If he had spare time, he needed to advertise or make deals to attract more customers. His daughter's family deserved nothing less. My grandfather would not allow my father to be right. When my father said white, the he said black; when my father said black, he said white. As far as I was concerned, he earned the name "the old bastard" because he was just that mean to my father.

Edwin Bourne
My Grandfather

I witnessed their arguing multiple times as I sat upstairs, eavesdropping. I even imitated my grandfather, holding my finger up, shaking it at my sister and saying "Now Sarah, you know, you need to be fair to your customers, but you are there to make money. Stop being chummy with them. You can't make money if you aren't aggressive.

TO ENDURE – REKINDLED LOVE

You are such an idiot if you think that listening to your clients is the way to make money. You know better than your clients. You need rules for them to follow. Stop being such a fool."

Finally, after I'd emptied my merciless berating on her, she'd had enough. She abruptly turned and ran to her room crying her eyes out. She stopped me cold, and I realized how offensive I became.

I thought she understood that I only mocked our grandfather. I thought she would laugh and urge me on like in the past. She did not. Grandmother came running up the stairs when she heard Sarah crying. Both Grandmother and Mother severely scolded me. Mother spanked me until I hurt from head to toe and shoved me into my dark room for the rest of the evening. I could only fume about my grandfather until I cried myself to sleep.

The next morning Mother came up to check on me. I'd slept on the floor all night in my clothes, without any covers over me. I awoke sad, angry, and disoriented. I remained frustrated things were not resolved.

I vowed I would not let anyone talk to me like my grandfather talked to Dad. I needed to hold my head up and never let on how I really felt. I would be assertive and state my point. I would charge forward in life, give it all I had, and never look back.[24]

****

---

[24] Part of my success in life was my resolve to keep my head above the fray and not allow myself to be tempted to do what I knew would be wrong. Nothing since has triggered my anger, as the anger I felt that evening.

Larry Calkins

Our fledgling family generally enjoyed life together when not confronted by the elder Bourne. In the 1920's, the stock market boomed. It appeared prosperity had no end in sight for us, and we planned to enjoy it. My father, as a stockbroker, made a good income, and he felt secure in his financial situation.

The stock market continued one of the best runs in its history in 1929. Between 1928 and the first nine months of 1929, it seemed like each week a new high occurred in the Dow Jones Average. From 1924 to the first part of 1929, a few economic downturns occurred, but overall, stocks rose, fueling speculation, moving the stock prices up rapidly. By placing a mere 10-20% down on stocks with a promise to pay off the original price at a later time, it seemed possible to sell at a substantial profit. When stock values would rise so rapidly, the stocks were paid off quickly, and there seemed to be ample cash flowing through the market rapidly.

Buying on the margins involved risk. At any time, a "margin call" could occur where the broker would request full payment of the stock. Great optimism thrived during this time, and most felt the risk remained worth it. Additionally, stocks were purchased on credit, called installment buying. Like purchasing a car or a refrigerator, investors placed a small amount down and paid a weekly, monthly, or yearly payment. Many purchased stocks on credit, even when they couldn't make the monthly payment. But, as the stocks rose, they also could be sold, costs recovered, profits made, and everyone benefited.

Dad could not understand the extreme speculation in the market. He thought extreme speculators would lose their shirts, especially if the market corrected itself, and he wanted to be a little more conservative

TO ENDURE – REKINDLED LOVE

than that. He believed the market would go up at a consistent rate, but intuitively felt that the market was undergoing unreasonable rate increases. It did not stop him from helping his clients speculate on the margins. But, he wanted to provide more solid investment advice for his clients. He, himself, invested in stocks he could afford, and stocks that had a solid track record. He also wanted to hedge his bets with more conservative investments in case the market did correct itself. Dad tried to base his portfolio on a wide range of investments.

Still, to appease his father-in-law, he started speculating too, despite his intuition. He purchased a few stocks on the margin, ones he felt were sure-fire investments that would make money back quickly. He began these speculative ventures late in 1927. He, like so many, did not foresee the unsustainable huge bubble in the market being created.

In addition to speculators making unsound purchases, businesses also began producing or manufacturing large quantities of products. Times were good and there seemed to be no shortage of people wanting to buy goods. Prices for these goods soared, while wages remained relatively constant. The recipe spelled ultimate disaster for business.

****

1929, a big profit year for Dad, allowed him to splurge on a major summer vacation. It seemed like we would continue in luxury. We did not need to rely on the Bourne family for a place to visit for our vacation.

That summer, we spent a long vacation on the north side of Cape Cod, near East Dennis, Massachusetts. Dad rented a small cottage as part of a large piece of shore land called the Swett's Estate. We had a half mile of private beach to play on and a nice cottage to live in. It included a stretch of beautiful curving beach with shallow water, extending out in front of the cottage for a long way, especially at low tide. The large, white Swett's home could be seen off to the east on a knoll, a good distance away from the cottage, but visible to us.

That summer, the Cape endured a heavy Nor'easter. During the storm hundreds of lobsters were swept in close to shore. We kids could walk out in waist-high water, and being careful where we stepped, see them at close range.

As Dad carefully picked up a lobster, he showed it to Sarah and me. "Sady, look at this. Those claws if they get ahold of you can hurt. I wonder how they would taste boiled up? What do you think?"

Sarah and I were excited to try something new, and we savored a delicious dinner of lobster. Our family decided then and there that lobster dinners would be a family favorite.

Dad, Sarah and me
Cape Cod

The same summer, the Swett's sold their place and held a big furniture auction, which Dad helped to organize. Dad also purchased from the estate several nice antiques, among them a pair of "spool" beds, which Dad scraped down to the bare pine. They adorned our spare bedroom for years.[25]

---

[25] Many years later, I found an identical spool bed at an auction in Seattle. Of course, I couldn't resist and bought it.

TO ENDURE – REKINDLED LOVE

Sarah, a little older and mobile, kept up with me like the best of them. We spent much time outside, playing many imaginative adventures, including going toward, but not in, the water. If Dad and Mother wanted some time together, they simply told Sarah and me to go outside, and we would play for hours. Often, Nurse Winifred went with us. We had the time of our lives.

Garbo ran off that summer. We didn't know what happened; maybe he got lost, maybe someone picked him up and liked him more than we did, or maybe someone shot him when he got into their garbage. Whatever happened, Garbo didn't come home one night. Sadness overtook us all.

Later that summer, we acquired a new German Shepard called Bexo. Bexo joined in our family fun, tiring us out as we ran after him. He stayed with us on the beach and at the cottage. It seemed like the summer of 1929 would never end.

***

Life improved at Grandmother's when our grandfather was gone or I found other things to do. I did not see our grandfather except in the evenings. Dad's fondness of football rubbed off on me and prodded me to learn how to play. I remembered the stories of the Yale ballgames he told about. My uncles, Mother's brothers,

Me and my football

Larry Calkins

Rich and Edwin Jr. (known as Rich and "E"), taught me how to play the game. The uncles played like kids themselves. They adored me and I them. We ran around in the back yard, tossing the football, tackling each other, and I learned how to block Rich and "E". We frolicked in a rough and tumble manner, but they always kept an eye out to protect me.

Joe was the oldest of Edwin's and Emma's children. Margaret was next in line, and admired by her younger brothers. Rich, born a year and half after Mother, sported athletic abilities more than others in the family. Edwin, four years younger than Mother, held the same name as his father and was the baby of the family. Rich and young "E" liked playing with me, and Rich became very much of a hero to us kids. Joe usually did his own thing and was not as sociable as his brothers.

Joe, as the oldest and respected head of Mother's immediate family, had a sense of duty and responsibility and did not fool around like his two younger brothers. All the boys felt warm affection toward my mother, especially Rich and "E". They had decided when my mother was engaged, that if Giles, became their sister's husband, they were going to be friendly with him and had since accepted their brother-in-law as part of the family. They did not give a hang what their mother and father said. They came over on Sunday nights, and we had a good time. When my grandfather was not around, tensions would clear up quickly.

***

Periodically, my parents took us to New York City to visit my Aunty Lucile. Dad's youngest sister, ten years his junior, took care of my paternal Grandmother, Ida Calkins (Dear Nana). Lucile married Ernest Moncrieff. Uncle Ernie supported his family quite well in New York.

TO ENDURE – REKINDLED LOVE

Upon our visit, the Moncrieff's welcomed our family in their large home in a loving and respectful way. Lucile fondly looked up to my father as the head of the Calkins family, now that their father had passed. The family reunions were a joyous occasion because my father's family had scattered to the three corners of the U.S. Katherine Balch (Aunty Kay), eight years younger than my father, lived in Los Angles. She had moved with her husband Clark Balch to pursue careers in sunny California.

Dear Nana, my father's mother, suffered with serious dementia and could not remember much of anything short-term. We fondly called her Dear Nana, an affectionate term Dad insisted we use. Dear Nana depended totally on the good will of Aunt Lucile and stayed cooped up in the apartment. Every once in a while, Aunt Lucile took her mother for a walk, talking to her and encouraging her to stay active. Lucile felt the sole burden of caring for Dear Nana and saw no reprieve in sight, but, when we visited, we brought relief. Aunt Lucile had others to talk to, especially those who cared about Dear Nana and her wellbeing and we were able to entertain Dear Nana and give Lucile a break.

Drawing "My Mother"
by Giles Calkins
(Dear Nana)

Dear Nana, a gentle soul, never meant any harm. She had been living for 76 years by the time I really got to know her.[26] Although she could not remember what we told her, she was always curious about Sarah and me. She continually asked how old we were, where we lived,

---

[26] She lived for another six years with dementia.

what we did, if we had any friends, and who they were. We would explain the best we could, but Dear Nana, a patient woman, always came back to a question she had asked previously. It seemed like she kept forgetting we were her grandchildren, and I came away heartbroken after talking to her, usually giving up.

Being a rambunctious six years old, I did not comprehend the gravity of the situation. I would follow Dear Nana around the house and make faces behind her back to get my sister to laugh. Sarah thought I made hilarious faces, and her response prompted me to continue.[27] I viewed it as fun and something to do to pass the time as the adults talked. Dear Nana would walk the house, back and forth, looking for things. Always looking for things. Initially polite, I tried to ask Dear Nana what she looked for, but I always got the same answer: "her hairbrush." So, I found it difficult talk to Dear Nana, because she would do the same things or ask me the same questions over and over. I loved Dad, and therefore it followed that I loved Dear Nana, his mother.

I never knew my grandfather, Travis G. Calkins, but the family told me stories about him and Dear Nana. Travis passed long before my birth, but he displayed a gentleness and fit nicely with the personality of my grandmother. Both of them attempted investing in the stock market. My grandfather worked hard developing other business ventures with his brothers becoming successful. He put the income from his business ventures to use in the stock market. Aside from gold and silver mines, he invested in telephone and telegraph companies and a boiler manufacturing company. The boiler manufacturing company did well,

---

[27] These frivolous actions bother me now because they were so uncaring, and I wish I could go back and change it.

TO ENDURE – REKINDLED LOVE

and that stock carried his ventures. Dear Nana also continued to invest and that helped the Moncrief family care for her through a power of attorney with Aunt Lucile.

***

In the 1920s, liquor could not be manufactured or sold at this time due to prohibition laws. Liquor entered New England as illegal, often bootlegged, liquor by organized crime and by store owners who simply ignored the law. To get around the illegal nature, local businesses set up "speak-easies" and they risked their business if caught by the authorities. Still, selling liquor continued to be lucrative, and local stores and bars trusted their customers. But, to buy or sell liquor, you needed to know someone. The businesses that operated speakeasies kept a close eye on those who they let in and only allowed in good friends or well-held and well-connected acquaintances. The small towns of Waban and New Bedford ran on connections. It became the only safe way to conduct business if you sold liquor.

Both my father, through his business contacts, and Mother, through her family in New Bedford, knew people who could set them up with a drink and a place to talk with other likeminded people. It became a society within a society, and my parents had the connections. They never talked about going to these places, mainly out of respect for the business owners who let them in, but they knew where to go for a good time. Good times seemed to continue with no end in sight.

On certain weekends, sometimes my parents left us kids with my grandfather and Grandmother or Nurse Winifred, and went dancing or to a local speak-easy for entertainment. Mother liked to have a little "nip" in the afternoon to take the edge off of the day. This pattern of behavior carried into the weekend. Father and Mother did not mind slipping into a speak-easy, to kick off their shoes and strike up conversations with good friends. Neither of my parents thought much about prohibition, and felt fairly safe going into such places. Still they were cautious to maintain the reputation both were struggling to build. Mother did not want to destroy her father's reputation. They just needed to be able to blow off a little steam once in a while.

They were discrete and never drank too much or caused too much of a fuss either inside or outside of the speakeasy. The dangers of being caught were real, especially in a small town where people gossiped. Most folks did not care, but some of the more self-righteous individuals could make life miserable for certain people if they wanted to. Reputations could be destroyed by one foolish mistake. Neither Father nor Mother wanted that to happen, for their sake and their family's sake. They carefully wandered their way through these moral dilemmas to be able to enjoy themselves on the weekend. This time of joy also demanded caution and prudency. Times were good, but they could not be too good.

TO ENDURE – REKINDLED LOVE

Chapter 7 – The Great Depression

During the 1920s, up until 1929, the nation's economy doubled in size. This period known as the roaring 20s, saw the large-scale use of automobiles, telephones, motion pictures, radio, and electronics. Wild investment speculation and risky business practices occurred during this time, and it seemed that everyone wanted a piece of the action. Instead of airplanes just being dreamed about, now businesses were getting into the aviation business flying customers from point "A" to "B." In the aftermath of World War I (at that time known as the Great War), art, jazz, and dancing rose in popularity.

People used their extra cash to indulge themselves, and the desperation that once plagued the country, dissolved. Mass production allowed the common person to obtain affordable goods. Except for the agricultural and coal mining sectors, the economy seemed to lift all boats on the rising tide, and each economic sector seemed to do well. Factories produced more goods than they could sell betting on future sales. Consumer confidence excelled. Even though wages barely rose, individuals felt they could extend their credit. Society bought goods and services in abundance, and everyone wanted some sort of stock portfolio from millionaires to health care workers, from teachers to cooks and even janitors. Some lived beyond their means, relying heavily on the future.

My father positioned himself to oblige and capitalize on all of this activity. As a stockbroker, he learned on the job, sought out lucrative deals, and shared his knowledge with his clients. He earned a substantial salary and had a decent portfolio himself. He liked the adventure of putting money into stocks and seeing his money rise. If he made some money on the side, it confirmed he did the right thing. He focused on several key stocks, speculating, but continually watched to see if he needed to sell part of his portfolio. His clients appreciated his candor and insight into the stocks they purchased or intended to buy. When they asked him to speculate on stocks or to purchase on credit or the margins, he suggested they be cautious. He wanted them to have sound investments. He called it the science of investing. My father alerted his clients when he felt a particular stock had played out and encouraged them to sell. He invested in the market similar to how he advised his clients.

More importantly, he continued to be interested in their lives, what they did for a living, and how their families were progressing. He experienced their personal successes and failures. In short, he became good friends with his clients. His success bred more success. His clients liked him, and, by word of mouth, his list of clients grew. Toward the end of the roaring 20s, he kept quite busy, working long hours, trying to keep up with his clients' needs.

August 1929, became the peak of prosperity in the stock market, and my father, along with many others, were caught flat footed, not wanting to believe the market had peaked. If he had sold his holdings in August, and encouraged others to sell, he and his clients would have

TO ENDURE – REKINDLED LOVE

been rich.

We kids spent the rest of the summer enjoying our freedom. We camped, played in the back yard, and swam in the local swimming hole. I went back to school in September and Sarah started preschool with little thought of our father's fate or the effect it would have on our family unit.

On October 24, 1929, it began to happen. The stock market started its crash. Nervous investors pulled money out of the stock market. There had been signs of a weakening economy as consumer spending started to slow, goods were being stockpiled, and production ground to a halt. It could have just been a short-term market correction. My father decided to ride it out. He, like so many people of the time, did not see the handwriting on the wall. He sold a few stocks but had faith in the system keeping most of his favorite stocks.

Within five days—on October 29th—the stock market officially crashed. This date became known as "Black Tuesday." It surprised my father how fast things happened. In panic mode, my father called all his clients and strongly suggested they sell their holdings. He did too. We did not see Dad for most of that week as he tried to salvage what income he could. He began selling stocks to pay his debts from other stocks he purchased on margin. The stocks he bought on margin tanked, but my father still owed the initial price on the stocks. To make matters worse, many of his clients blamed him for their loss in the market. Only a few of his loyal customers kept with him. My father was devastated by his loss of the stocks and the money he expected the stocks to make; but more importantly devastated by the loss in the relationships, reputation and credibility he had spent years in building. Friendships strained under the financial losses; years of relationships ended.

Larry Calkins

My father became unsure of himself and fought to keep his good humor. He could not bear the loss of his good friends and clients that put their trust in him all these years. He did the best he could at the time, gave the best advice, and acted responsibly. However, it did not seem to mollify his deep hurt and sadness. That week not only deeply impacted him, but affected the whole country.

President Hoover tried to reassure America the economic downturn could be only a temporary setback and the country could rebound financially. My father took that to heart, hoping for the best and responding to his clients in the same way. However, the country did not rebound.[28]

My father's clients disappeared daily as they lost money in the stock market. He quickly became one of the casualties of the Great Depression. While many clients knew he had no control over the situation, they simply had no money to continue as his client. Mother, and, to a lesser extent us kids, felt our hearts wrenched seeing him come home, not say much, and just head straight to bed. I don't remember many nights where he even ate dinner.

I heard Dad say, "Maybe Edwin knew what he talked about, after all."

I wanted to cry out, "NO, that guy doesn't know anything."

---

[28] By 1930, four million Americans had lost their jobs; the country's production reduced to half. By 1931, the number of unemployed Americans rose to over eight million, or sixteen percent. Before it ended in 1933, one quarter of the population lacked employment.

TO ENDURE – REKINDLED LOVE

Instead, I just kept quiet and felt his sadness and loss of control over his situation.

No one had control. My grandfather, Edwin, invested solely in local New Bedford stock. He kept absolute faith in New Bedford, but the Depression wiped him out. The city he knew and trusted began to fall apart. The textile mills were laying people off. The life he expected to continue just the way it had always been could not sustain itself. As he struggled to pay off the heavy speculation he had been invested in, my father still provided an easy outlet for my grandfather's frustrations.

Over the years, my grandmother, Emma, accumulated wealth by saving a portion of her household budget every month, as well as funds inherited/gifted by her father, family and friends. Her brother and father had made plenty of money during the 1920s, and my grandmother received dividends and payments, including a substantial inheritance when her father passed away. She considered it her money, keeping it separate, and the family called it Emma's money[29]. She had the foresight to wisely invest during the "good" years in secure stocks and bonds that typically provided reasonable rates of dividends and interest. Her choice of stocks included utilities and large cap stocks with a solid record of performance, and she purchased them outright.

During the Depression, my grandmother's stocks held up. She lost some money too, but nothing compared to others, especially her

---

[29]My grandfather lost so much that he and Grandmother survived solely on her money. When the family fortune diminished and eventually became completely wiped out during the Great Depression of the 1930's, she helped keep the ship afloat with her savings.

husband.

Joe and Rich, who also worked in the financial industry like my dad, also played the margins and bought stock on credit. They ended up losing quite a bit as well. Young Edwin did as he darn well pleased, so he became a salesman of some sort. He made a little money and got along. The other ones, fortunately had wives that were better off than they (likely from their ties to their families of origin), so they were able to survive.

Mother, a strong-willed person as she is, held our family together. At only seven or eight years old, I knew what happened. I understood enough to know that my father had fallen into real trouble, and I expressed concern about him.

Mother use to say that the Great Depression affected me deeply. I really did not see it that way, other than it affected my dad, and whatever affected my dad affected me. We knew the adults struggled during the Depression. The Great Depression changed my father's life. It bothered me that his inability to make money to support his family took his self-esteem to rock bottom. His lack of self-esteem broke me—not our financial situation.

Fortunately, Dad's well-to-do sister, Aunt Lucile (fondly called Aunty Cile) periodically fed him some money. Luckily, she helped him, otherwise life would have been much more of a fight to make ends meet. My father's depressed state of mind occurred because he, like all stockbrokers, were not making money. We struggled for at least seven or eight years.

Dad continued to be pestered by the Bourne's. The Bourne's saw

TO ENDURE – REKINDLED LOVE

his struggles in keeping his brokering relationships as a sign of weakness.[30]

But, I did not regret it; I think it hardened me. I came from a soft family setting. Mother watched herself carefully, always concerned about appearances. She believed that the family must stay strong in the face of adversity; lots of adversity occurred during the Depression. Because Mother grew up babied, the Depression provided the push for her to become stronger and develop the starch to handle a crisis; and she learned to trudge through it, a crisis for all of America really. People were hungry all over the country between 1930 and 1940.

I did not want to cross any of the Bourne's. I kept a low profile. My cousins, Tanny and Rusty, Joe's kids, always admired me, and I enjoyed their company as well even though I was a little older than both of them. Their parents never belittled me nor said "don't pay any attention to your older cousin." They respected me. Sarah, being two and a half years younger and not as tied to our father, did not understand the financial situation or the torment he suffered. She interacted with them just fine, being not nearly as affected as I was.

My parents did their best to keep the family unit together and work though their difficulties. I attended school at a Waban Elementary school, and my sister began school there too. I made friends, but avoided the children whose parents were clients of Dad's. Some were particularly vicious and taunted me ferociously. In trying to avoid them, and on more than one occasion, I came home angry because of the day's events.

---

[30] New Englanders think that unless you're making money, you're no damn good.

Larry Calkins

Mother comforted me and told me not let these mean boys get the better of me. Down deep inside, I knew it was because they scrapped by and readjusted their lifestyle, just like I did. Their parents endured enormous stress, just like my parents. They often had a harder time than my family.

My sister, Sarah, may have struggled in a different way. I was finding my own way and found it hard to advise her. Both Mother and Dad used the old English adage, "Keep a stiff upper lip." In context, I knew it meant, "Don't let these things bother you, and keep on going no matter what the cost." That became the only advice I had at the time, and I took it to heart. Consequently, I tried to ignore those mean boys and develop new friendships on my own. Eventually, the assaults subsided, and I made my way through school without interference.

***

My sister, Sarah, tells a story about our Quaker family. She obtained some money during the depression and experienced a moralistic lesson. Sarah explained the story emphasized the frugal upbringing she had and Quaker values.

> One day, a nice lady gave me a nickel for doing some kind deed. I think she must have felt sorry for me. I was so happy! I purchased a porcelain dog with puppies. Being very so proud of the purchase, I showed it to Grandfather. Grandfather sternly chastised me for the purchase and for not saving the nickel. It had a lasting impression on me.
>
> *Sarah Calkins-Palmer*

***

The Waban house lay on the outskirts of Boston. It was comfortable and suited our family with its three bedrooms and one bath.

TO ENDURE – REKINDLED LOVE

One warm summer day, Casey Squires, Mother's friend who visited until my birth came to visit Mother again in 1930. As a schoolteacher, she thought nothing about driving to see Mother and her family. Casey liked the adventure. Mother told me to give up my room so Casey could be comfortable. I slept in a sleeping bag on the floor or on the living room couch. It bothered me to give up my room, but I wanted to please Mother, so I did it without much complaint.

Mother graciously accepted Casey, as always. Casey's mannerisms and speech patterns seemed odd and eventually became annoying.[31] Unfortunately, neither Sarah nor I were interested in spending time with her, so Casey and Mother talked every day, for a month. Casey had to be back in Evanston, Illinois, to teach school in September. When Casey left I happily got my room back.

As Dad complained, "Casey just doesn't know when to leave. I wondered if she ever would," Sarah and I giggled at the thought.

***

Father found it difficult to go into Boston every day to work. As difficult as it was to continue his routine, he had a family to support and he kept hoping that somehow the stock market would pick up and that he could once again salvage his business. He just went through the motions, attempting to hold it together often coming home early. He did not really have a choice; he could not find employment elsewhere. He tried but to no avail. Even with his degree, he could not get an engineering job because there were no openings. Engineers he knew from Yale either

---

[31] Casey's mother died in the 1960s and she found a nice man to marry. She began to display a more sophisticated personality.

kept their engineering jobs, kept whatever job they had or were unemployed. Dad had little to do. The stocks he kept, depreciated to a pittance of what they once were. At times, he would cash them in just to keep the family afloat. Our savings disappeared. His clientele thinned to a few loyal clients, but they too lost a lot and were trying to keep food on the table. He would not eat much at night, saying he wanted to save the food for the children. He would often retire early to bed.

Dad had several customers, one a butcher. We enjoyed pretty good meat during the depression. The butcher was able to purchase stock because he had another source of income, possibly an inheritance or a side business. Before the Depression, he bought quite a bit from Dad. During the Depression, Dad did not sell much, and what he did sell, he did not make a commission. Those were the days where no-one purchased anything and to make ends meet, the barter system returned.

One day, Dad came home with a pig under his arm. Sarah and I tried to refrain from laughing, but first a snicker slipped out of Sarah, then I started to giggle too, then we just outright laughed. The pig's comic relief released our inhibitions. It was hilarious the way Dad held the pig as it squealed and squirmed, trying to escape. He did his best to maintain his death grip on the pig, but Dad became no match for the squirmy pig. I had no idea how he got it on the train, let alone rode all the way from work to home with it. He explained that his client had no cash and wanted to keep his stocks, but had no way to pay for the fees. My father bartered with him, and the client suggested the idea of the pig. Mother did not express her happiness, but she instead told Dad to take the pig straight to the butcher, and, at least, we would have meat on the table for the next week. I could see the grin peeking through as she told

TO ENDURE – REKINDLED LOVE

him that. Mother knew if that pig stayed in our house that it would become a family pet, and we needed food far more right now. Mother knew the gravity of the situation and knew her husband made the best deal possible. My father needed to keep his few remaining clients, and we needed food on the table, and this was definitely a win-win.

***

We ended up losing our home in Waban. Dad could not pay the mortgage and other bills. My parents were determined to make the best of a bad situation, but he and Mother looked long and hard for a home they could afford and finally settled on one in Marshfield. Even though the commute became longer, my father had already lost the clientele he once had and valued the additional time to travel by train, a place where he could relax. Marshfield, a town at the end of the train's commuter route, allowed us to enjoy country living. It also made Mother happy because Marshfield's location made travel to her parent's home in New Bedford easier. If times got tougher, she could visit her mother more often.

My Aunty Lucile (Cile) placed herself right in the middle of things. Her husband, Ernie, a big guy on Wall Street, made quite a lot of money. They came down from New York and visited our family every once in a while. Aunty Cile acted childlike, very overdramatic about everything she did. She quoted poetry and appeared theatrical in her description of things. She and Mother did not get along worth a darn and really disliked each other. But Aunty Cile came around anyway because she remained fond of her brother. Mother got her emotional and financial support from her side of the family. Aunty Cile gave Dad support from his side. So, Aunty Cile balanced things out in a way. As much as Aunty

Cile loved her brother, she could only stay with us so long since she still had social obligations in New York. Dad gratefully accepted her support, both emotionally and financially.

For Sarah and me, moving included adventure. We explored our new surroundings. My parents seemed happier in Marshfield. My father resigned himself to his loss of clients. We appreciated the country with its affordable housing and beautiful surroundings. We took long walks, reminiscent of a time we used to get to be with Dad on the weekends. Mother joined us sometimes, Dad's stories returned, and the artwork began again. Dad became content with the routine. I don't think he missed the hustle and bustle of the 1920s. Having lost the house in Waban, we readjusted further to having little to no money. Mother began growing a garden. Sarah and I helped her, from planting to weeding to harvesting. We also helped out around the house, keeping it clean and doing dishes. I hated dishes, but Mother said it "built character" and that I needed to do them anyway. I often washed, and Sarah dried. I would have rather pushed the vacuum around the house or swept. Being in the country, some part of the house always seemed to need sweeping. Whenever I did not know what to do or got into trouble, mother handed me the broom and told me that I knew what needed to be done.

At school in Marshfield, the children of my father's former clients did not antagonize me because his clients lived in Boston; a blessing for me. Sarah seemed to bloom in this environment. The fresh start and new expectations thrived in the fresh air of the country.

TO ENDURE – REKINDLED LOVE

Sarah and I got our bicycles in Marshfield. Another one of my father's clients, like the owner of the pig, fell on hard times, and his children had two bicycles. Dad traded fees for the bicycles so we would have some form of transportation that was, at least, quicker than walking. Even Mother liked the bicycles. She could tell us to go to the local market or to a neighbor's home to get some eggs, milk or bread. We never ate like kings or queens during the Depression, but we usually enjoyed, at least, two square meals a day. Mother assured that we had the basic things we needed. She learned how to be more self-sufficient and taught us children to do the same.

Sarah and Travis Calkins our bicycles and the Packard

Once in a while, Dad proudly displayed the old Packard because it remained a symbol of affluence. Mostly though, it remained in the garage. No one could afford to drive anywhere. Basics like food and shelter continued to be the primary expenses during the depression, with gas being a luxury.

On another occasion, my father traded fees for a goat. Sarah and I thought highly of that idea. We drank goat's milk for a number of years. At the end, I yearned for good old cow's milk, but, eventually, I gave up milk altogether, drinking water instead.

Larry Calkins

A picture is said to be worth a thousand words. Picture, if you will, our old rooster in the coldest freeze of the century in Marshfield, Massachusetts in 1935. Mother and I, at about eleven years old, went out to feed the hens, and there was the old rooster, lying on the floor of the henhouse, alert, but prone, unable to stand on his frozen legs. Mother picked him up carefully, took him to the kitchen with its coal-fired range, and placed him behind it in a large parrot cage. Within a half hour the rooster paraded around the house, clucking and crowing, apparently none the worse for wear. Mother didn't seemed surprised at all. In fact, we ate him not to long after that.

The Old Rooster

Sometimes in Marshfield we could not even afford the basics. My father tried hard to barter, earn an income, or come up with other ways to provide for his family. But some months were harsh. He just could not bring in the income needed or develop the wherewithal to deliver the kind of resources a family needs to survive. My father's line of business became completely obsolete as the depression waned on.

Bread lines and soup lines increased in number, especially in the cities. But, even in Marshfield, neighbors found resources to provide for a soup line. As humbling as that experience was, my father stood in some of those lines and somehow food found its way back to our family.

The Great Depression occurred roughly from 1929 to 1939. The crisis dominated my childhood and undoubtedly played a part in most of our family activities. Mother's strong survival instincts and great mental toughness were put to the test again and again as we struggled through difficult economic stress. Her mental frame of mind of "onward and upward" showed in the raising of a bountiful vegetable garden and a flock of Rhode Island Red hens. She whipped Dad back into shape as he recovered from the shock of losing everything in 1929 and 1930. She added to the family income from her ladies' knitting club which brought in a few needed bucks in tough times. Mother sent us kids door to door, selling eggs, and Grandmother Bourne helped with checks from her own bank account from time to time.

While we all decried the tough times, and lambasted the Democrats as the villains, who were the cause of all our troubles, Mother forbade wallowing in self-pity over our misfortune. A certain bitterness presented itself in our thinking, but circumstances demanded action, not hand-wringing. When times are tough, the tough get going. That unspoken philosophy prevailed, and we knew we would survive. The family convinced itself that Roosevelt and the Democrats would "get theirs."

The Depression included a time of bank runs and loss in confidence of all financial institutions. If banks did opened up, a long line of people stood outside to withdraw all their money. Many banks needed to close because they no longer had cash on hand, let alone enough to invest. Banks needed to liquidate loans to supplement their meager cash reserves. In the fall of 1930, the first of a wave of Bank runs occurred. Investors lost confidence in the solvency of their financial institutions and wanted their money while the bank had money. Other bank runs occurred in the spring and fall of 1931, the fall of 1932 and again in 1933. The Hoover Administration decided to prop up some of the banks by providing them with federal loans.

When the public elected Franklin Roosevelt in 1933, we visited the Bourne's and they blamed Roosevelt for everything going wrong with their lives. The Bourne's thought Roosevelt spent too much of their tax money on creating work projects. They thought Roosevelt and the federal government regulated and meddled in the private affairs of the banks and other financial institutions too much, although, they didn't seem to mind Federal monies coming to the banks to prop them up. They fiercely objected to Roosevelt cracking down and creating too many suffocating regulations for the banking industry and financial industries. Our family could not appreciate the Roosevelt Administration as they tried to stabilize the economy and avoid large boom and then bust cycles[32].

The true cause of the Great Depression eluded our family as being the result of a laisse-faire policy. Roosevelt felt financial transactions needed boundaries to prevent a future event like October 1929.

President Franklin D. Roosevelt, FDR, had been classmates with Frederic Howland Taber, or FH for short, at Harvard in 1904. FH, Uncle Fred's son, attended to law school at Harvard and opened a law practice in New Bedford. He was my Mother's cousin, albeit 17 years older than she. FH shared in Uncle Fred's businesses, including serving on the board of my grandfather's bank and the Taber Textile Mill. The success of his father, Uncle Fred, as a Bank President, the Chair of the Boards at the Bank and the Textile Mills resulted in FH becoming known as the "million dollar baby"[33] to the family. FH, Uncle Fred's only son, stood to

---

[32] When I became older and reviewed the events of the 1930s, I found that how Roosevelt resolved the depression merited rethinking.
[33] "Million Dollar Baby" information provided by Tanny Bourne, my Cousin)

TO ENDURE – REKINDLED LOVE

inherit all his father's wealth.

The Roosevelt Administration attempted to be problem solvers. As the Depression rolled into full swing, FDR recruited his old classmate, FH, to become one of the Directors[34] of the Reconstruction and Finance Corporation (RFC) from 1933 to 1937.[35]

The U. S. Government owned and operated the RFC, but established it as an independent agency. The agency played a major role in recapitalizing U.S. Banks, and it effectively reduced bank failures and stimulated bank lending. It also set up relief programs that became a part of the New Deal in 1933. It had broad bipartisan support in Congress.

Roosevelt with FH's help increased RFC's funding, streamlined the bureaucracy, and stabilized prosperity for business interests, especially with the banking and railroad industries. The New Deal expanded the RFC's power to purchase bank stock and extend loans for agriculture, housing, exports, business and government entities, and disaster relief.

34

https://fraser.stlouisfed.org/files/docs/publications/rcf/rfc_19590506_finalreport.pdf

35

http://www.fdrlibrary.marist.edu/archives/collections/franklin/index.php?p=collections/findingaid&id=201

The RFC conducted its business without oversight by Congress, so it became very efficient. The RFC set up electric and gas entities for farm families in rural areas as well as offered crop assistance to tide them over through the depression years.

> The first six months of the present administration, beginning with the date of inauguration of President Roosevelt in March 1933, was a period of hopefulness and encouragement. The Hoover Administration had ended in an atmosphere of constantly increasing discouragement. For the past three years since the panic of 1929, the business and financial fabric of this country had become more and more shattered…. The incoming administration from its inception enjoyed the confidence of almost everyone. It promised a change from what had immediately preceded it. For this reason it was regarded hopefully and during the six months period referred to it did not disappoint its most ardent partisans. Probably this period will be considered as one of the most constructive periods in our history.
>
> *Frederic H. Taber,*
> *A Board Director of RFC*
> *My mother's older cousin*

FH helped direct the agency and became a key contributor to helping America work its way out of the depression. Under FH's[36] direction and the Franklin Roosevelt's administration, the RFC implemented basic reconstruction programs to pull America up by its bootstraps, once again.

---

[36] I wish I asked my Grandfather about FH, "the million dollar baby," and his relationship with the Democrats and the RFC.

TO ENDURE – REKINDLED LOVE

Chapter 8 – Sadness

My father's lousy financial situation was similar to my grandfather's. One major difference, however, was that Dad knew he had financial trouble with little way out, and Grandfather could rely upon Grandmother. There were months where Dad could not pay the rent, even in Marshfield. There were more days where obtaining food became excruciatingly difficult. Simply providing for one's family seemed nearly impossible.

Dad displayed waves of feelings including loss and minor depression prior to our move to Marshfield, but he loved Marshfield. He had lost most of his clients and income and became depressed because he could not seem to get on his feet. We all loved Marshfield. It seemed, Dad started getting back to his old self even though the income was not there and enjoyed life again. Even though it would be an impossible task to predict, he could not help but question himself about how he missed signs that the market would drop so significantly and what he could have done differently. The Great Depression erased nearly everybody's lifelong earnings. Dad conducted himself in the most cautious manner he could, especially after he understood the seriousness of the Depression. He tried to make money but failed. How did he intend to feed his family?

He did not want to accept anyone else's help, including his extended family, but it became the only way out.

In discussing the situation with my dad, Mother finally put her foot down. She wanted her family provided for, even if it meant groveling to her parents. Her mother had squirrelled some savings away and built a small nest egg. My mother knew if she went to her father, he would gloat and say, "I told you so, and that husband of yours was a terrible choice." Mother decided to just confide in her mother, instead. Besides, her father had lost everything too.

Grandmother responded happily when asked. The least she could do for one of her family would be to provide something to tide them over. Mother didn't ask for much, just enough to get them by. She and her mother agreed on an amount, and Grandmother liquidated some from her stocks and savings and gave it to her. Mother appreciated the gift and left without saying a word to her father.

My family rejoiced when Mother returned, and those funds lasted us for a couple of months, while Dad still struggled to make ends meet. Everyone thought it would be a temporary situation; no one dreamed it would continue for as long as it did.

***

In 1935, Dad found a nice home in Hingham. The home, a duplex located right on Main Street, had a large front porch and included ample room for our family. He and Mother discussed it and decided it would be a better place for our family than the Marshfield house. The Marshfield house resembled unsophisticated country housing for their

TO ENDURE – REKINDLED LOVE

tastes, and Hingham reminded my mother of New Bedford. Hingham appeared to be more upscale and closer to Boston. Dad still daily took the train, but it became a slightly cheaper commute. Sarah and I viewed it as another adventure.

In Hingham, Uncle Joe and Aunty Silv came to visit us often. Joe married Aunty Silv and raised two children, Tanny and Rusty. My Uncle Joe happened to be the oldest and most self-assured of my grandfather and grandmother's children. Aunty Silv, a lovely,

> Travis mapped the big wet area where the creeks were behind the house and down into the town. This meant driving stakes and pacing off distances and taking angles with a protractor. There were still snow fields and ice flows in the area. Travis was just enough bigger than I so he could move faster and jump farther. I enjoyed myself but had a hard time keeping up with Travis. It was great fun to try."
>
> *Tanny*

self-effacing person, had a much different personality than Joe who was much more outgoing and gregarious. One wondered how she would ever marry a self-assured guy like Joe. I was fond of Aunty Silv partly due to her personality and partly because she was a close friend of my mother's as well as her brother's wife. I grew close to Tanny and Rusty. Tanny was Sarah's age and Rusty was a couple of years younger. My fondness grew for Tanny and Rusty in part because each were very polite individuals and were fun to be with. Tanny seemed to be always smiling, very friendly, and a little on the self-assured side. He knew where he belongs[37]. Tanny would run up to us with a little bounce in his step and a big smile and Rusty would follow.

---

[37] He comes from a family of bankers. His father, Joe, became a note broker and a banker, like our grandfather.

Larry Calkins

Growing up, I played well with both Tanny and Rusty[38]. The younger cousins entertained us, and Sarah and I adored them—consequently, we became leaders of our cousins. With me being the oldest, I normally headed the pack.

Tanny and I went swimming in a creek in the back of the Hingham house. The most memorable part of our swim was the "blood suckers" that we had to pull off of ourselves.

Tanny had a much better relationship with our Grandfather Bourne than I. Grandfather and Grandmother Bourne visited them in

> Grandfather Bourne took me for a ride in his car (all by myself; in the front seat, no less). I think he wanted to get out of the house so he could smoke a cigar. Grandfather always said he smoked White Owls and showed me how to remove the paper band first. He pulled out this neat little cigar clipper on his watch chain to cut a little piece out of the round end. Then, he inserted that end into an amber colored cigar holder and pushed in the cigar lighter on the dashboard. (Our car did not have a cigar lighter but Grandfather's did.) Then came the actual lighting, followed by clouds of aromatic smoke.
>
> By this time, Grandfather was retired, but we determined both Grandfather and Grandmother were very successful. In 1937, they had moved into this apartment in New Bedford at the Roosevelt Hotel, and they still had the cottage at Nonquitt. Additionally, every winter they took the train to Sarasota, Florida, and stayed there a few months.
>
> *Tanny*

Milton, MA. Grandfather took him on a joy ride and taught him how to smoke cigars.[39] Our Grandfather smoked White Owl cigars. I enjoyed the

---

[38] Rusty writes very well and in fact, writes for a living. He became an editor of American Heritage Books and an author of fascinating historic books such as "Cradle of Violence – Boston's Waterfront Mobs Ignited the American Revolution," "The View From Front Street," and "The Red King's Rebellion; Racial Politics in New England 1675-1678."

[39] I'm sure Grandfather never let Tanny smoke one but who knows?

TO ENDURE – REKINDLED LOVE

smell of his cigar smoke too[40], it reminded me of my father as he smoked either pipes or cigars.

Tanny visited Hingham in the early spring of 1937. Tanny and Rusty were farmed out to our family because their maternal grandmother died, and his folks needed to handle the funeral and estate details like selling the house. My parents agreed to take the boys in for a while. Tanny was ten; I was thirteen. Of course, I enjoyed being an avid boy scout and was working on my star rank. One of the requirements was to earn merit badges. As I worked on my "mapping merit badge," Tanny said he enjoyed tagging along behind as he tried to keep up with me.

One day, I took him to visit my friend, Buckie Brown. Buckie had the most elaborate and extensive electric train set-up in his cellar that anyone had ever seen.

The next summer, our family moved from Hingham to Fairhaven, near New Bedford. I visited Tanny's family for a while in Padanaram, a small town about ten miles south of New Bedford where they'd taken over the summer cottage belonging to his mother's parents. We did something stupid and got in trouble and ended up confined to his upstairs room, not able to go anywhere. When we then tried to even for being confined to the room by dropping noisemakers out of our window we got into more trouble. I was proud to be the instigator of that event.

---

[40] It was one reason I tried later in life to smoke cigars too.

> Somehow Travis, Rusty and I had been confined to my bedroom on the second floor which happened to be right over May's bedroom. May was a lovely girl about eight years older than me who came from Nova Scotia, who lived with my parents to cook and clean and take care of the kids.
>
> I don't remember exactly how it happened, but we were getting even with her by dropping firecrackers out my window. The firecrackers were timed to explode right outside her window, where she was getting a few minutes rest.
>
> *Tanny*

Mother remained available to help Tanny's family through the rough times, and my Uncle and Aunt tried to reciprocate.[41]

***

Things went fairly well in Hingham. With it being city living we did not have the walks and talks we enjoyed in Marshfield. Life became a little more stressful.

In 1936, Dear Nana, my father's mother, came to live with us. She had full dementia, by the time she stayed with us, and needed full time care. Mother did the caregiving. Then, she was hospitalized for an unknown illness. The Hingham newspaper simply stated, "Mrs. Giles Calkins of Main Street, Hingham, has been showing slight improvement

---

[41] Tanny felt his family got the best of the deal. But, I didn't agree. Jumping ahead in time when his father died in 1965, Mother went east for a couple of weeks to help Tanny's mother.

Incidentally many years later, both Tanny and I slept on twin beds in a nearby apartment, kindly loaned to us by one of Aunty Silv's friends who happened to be out of town for a few days. We hardly slept and talked most of the night reliving the stories like these. The next day we drove together to Hingham and New Bedford just to look around.

TO ENDURE – REKINDLED LOVE

at the hospital where she has been a recent patient." It was very likely she became depressed and subject to illness due to caregiving for her mother-in-law. Dear Nana, my dad's mother, required constant care, and the constant need strained Mother. Every time Mother left the house, she locked the doors and worried Dear Nana would leave the house too. The concern about her mother-in-law and demand of meeting her needs stressed and tired my mother.

By April Dear Nana passed away.

***

Mother also felt strain from a duty to provide for her family, and we had a difficult time financially. She resolved to go back to her parents to request more money to tide them over.

Dad still did not make any money. Mother pulled together what she could, but paying the bills became more and more difficult. The summer of that same year, Margaret knew what she had to do. She returned to her mother's home. Again, she asked for a small amount to tide them over. But, going back to the well on a repeated basis only asked for trouble.

The more my mother went to ask her parents, the more stressed Dad became. Coupled with his mother's passing, Dad found it difficult to make decisions. He had never experienced this kind of situation before. He feared he would lose his family.

For a final time, Mother felt she needed to go back to her parents and ask for money. My grandmother no longer kept things a secret from my grandfather. My grandfather initially became suspicious, but

Grandfather unleashed his fury when he found out my grandmother previously gave money to tide them over. He seriously talked to her about his daughter's situation. He wanted to have Mother file for divorce.

When Mother arrived, both her mother and father met her at the door. My grandmother, in a strong-willed voice, said "Margaret, I want you to divorce that man; he's lost all his money." They fully blamed my father.

My mother could not believe her ears. She should not be treated like a child anymore. She had effectively managed a family of her own. But, the more she stayed and listened to her parents, the more she saw the necessity of what they suggested. At least, she would be able to feed her children and keep the family unit together, with the exception of my father. Besides, my father relied on Lucile, and he could rely on her again. She always viewed a divorce more as a separation than a divorce. But the more she talked to her parents, the more convinced she became that divorcing Dad befitted her predicament. She went back to Hingham empty handed, but in the company of her parents. She planned on picking up her children and their belongings and taking them to the New Bedford area, specifically to nearby Fairhaven.

Divorce was uncommon in those days. She would begin a new life and a new paradigm. She did not have to like it, she needed to persevere and deal with her life. "Keep the stiff upper lip."

Although Mother got a divorce because her parents demanded it, she decided to be responsible for and committed to her children and her estranged husband. But, in order to do that, she needed to take things into

TO ENDURE – REKINDLED LOVE

her own hands.[42] Mother, when pressed, took on the complete responsibility for her two children. Her husband did not have the financial security her family needed. What else could she do? She didn't feel she had much of a choice.

When Margaret arrived in Hingham for the last time, Dad was in the back room. She entered with my grandparents. She quickly gathered up her belongings.

She told me, "Travis, pack up all your clothes and anything you can't live without. I'll come and get you in a few minutes. We will be leaving shortly."

She told Sarah to do the same. We were not told where we were going or why, just to get ready to leave. Mother went to the back room to talk to Dad. I could hear some loud talking, but was distracted by my grandparents urging me to hurry. It took about twenty minutes, but then we piled into the old man's car and headed toward New Bedford. Dad wanted to follow, but knew better. Mother had decided to follow through with the divorce to appease her parents.

Dad could not deal with it. He lost every morsel of his self-confidence. This time, Dad had a serious nervous breakdown that diminished his ability to do much of anything. He stopped going to work. He simply hid at the house. When Mother divorced him, he had no power left in him to fight and simply acquiesced. He fell into a deep, deep funk.

---

[42] I admire her for that, and think she did the right thing to take on this responsibility.

Larry Calkins

Leaving was so abrupt that I did not have time to process anything. I thought Dad would join us, and we could be a happy family again. That did not happen. The family continued to push the divorce action that Mother, herself, really did not want. But, Mother filled out the divorce paperwork, signed it, and began and finalized the divorce proceedings.

Dad drove himself even further into despair. By 1937, Dad, being banished from his family, finally realized that his inability to provide for them resulted in him losing them entirely. He had no fight left in him to negotiate, and no ability to offer anything to push toward reconciliation. Dad could not work. And now, what was the point? He stayed in bed for much of the next three weeks. When he came to grips with what had happened, he took the train into Boston one day to wrap up his business with the clients he could salvage.

A neighbor called on Dad in Hingham. He had not seen my father for a while and wondered about him. The two always enjoyed each other's company, and now Dad, uncharacteristically, stayed in the house, did not even go to work. When Dad answered the door, he seemed to speak gibberish. "My children are gone. I don't know anything about them anymore. I can't visit. I can't call. I'm stuck here. New Bedford's a long way away."

He rambled on about his children in New Bedford and how he did not know how it happened. The more the neighbor pried, the less he understood. Finally, the neighbor decided to help Dad. The neighbor found out about Lucile, Dad's sister who we called Aunty Cile, and purchase a bus ticket to New York so he could live with his sister.

TO ENDURE – REKINDLED LOVE

Since Giles made no money, he lived on the generosity of his sister. Her husband worked as a big oil man, so he provided Lucile with whatever she needed. They lived in a big house in New York. She gladly helped her brother. Lucile remained all caught up in New York high society. Her husband, the well to do businessman, had a stiff, self-centered type of demeanor that outwardly showed little emotion. His personality did not reflect it, but he took good care of his wife and his wife's brother and his family. His actions portrayed a generous man, type of guy who offered a place for a little kid like me to stay as part of his family and for any other member of his family, including his brother-in-law. He was a godsend. He gave us a boost showing his compassion though his actions.

***

Mother, Sarah and I lived near grandmother and grandfather. They owned a little house in Fairhaven that my grandfather had purchased before the Depression across the river from New Bedford. I enjoyed school for my seventh-grade in Fairhaven. Although I disliked my grandfather, my grandmother offered support to all of us and helped things run smoothly. Fortunately, she saw the wisdom of her daughter, her only daughter, having the love of her children and having family unity. During the middle of the school year, I decided to live with my Auntie Cile and Dad for about a month. I missed Mother and Sarah and decided to go back and finish up that year of my school in Fairhaven.

My father ended up checking himself into a mental hospital in New York for a short while to deal with his depression. It became a gut wrenching moment. He voluntarily locked himself away to deal with his anxiety about losing his family and employment.

Larry Calkins

My grandfather stayed at home with Emma, and I only had to deal with him periodically, when we saw our grandparents. I was happy we stayed in Fairhaven for the most part, although to reach New Bedford, we just needed to cross a bridge. We saw them more than I cared to, but we also had our own space to retreat to. My grandfather did not say much to me, but I knew I reminded him of my father, who he loathed. He did not need to say much, because his look, tone, and mannerisms when he spoke to me told me how he felt. But, my grandmother never seemed to display that nasty attitude toward us.

I initially thought his attitude only focused on me, but the Depression kept grinding away, and the old man's gruff demeanor was directed toward the rest of our family. He must have felt it was a burden to take care of me and my family, but he would rather have his daughter near New Bedford with her children, than for her to be with my father. By this time, he was aging and not feeling well.

Mother noticed I became sullen and thought I was affected by the Depression, but really it was my father's state of affairs that bothered me. I felt the impact of the Depression on my father, his divorce to my mother, and his loss of money, family and respect. I could not clearly express that, nor did I have the tools to deal with it at my age.

***

One day, toward the end of our living in Fairhaven, I looked out the window, and a figure stood outside my window, peering from the bushes. I could not believe my eyes.

I opened the window and asked, "Dad, what are you doing

TO ENDURE – REKINDLED LOVE

here?"

I knew that he should not be here. If he were caught, my grandfather would certainly have his way, call the cops, and Dad would be thrown in jail. Grandfather knew the local police chief well. Dad put his finger to his mouth and shushed me.

He whispered, "I really miss you kids, and I desperately wanted to see you. I really don't want any of the adults to know I stopped by. I wanted to see how you were doing and make sure you are well."

I ran to get Sarah. From the window, both Sarah and I were thrilled to see Dad. He said, "I'm still staying with Aunty Cile, but spent a little time in the hospital, and I'm trying to get my life back together again."

We tried to understand, but it did not make much sense to us. He became far more interested in how we were doing. He asked about school, if we had made friends, and what we did for fun. We answered him the best we could. He did not stay long, continually looking over our shoulders for the adults.

Finally, Dad gave both of us a kiss and said, "Be good." He disappeared quickly. The fact that he came to see us tenderly showed his integrity and love for Sarah and me.

Larry Calkins

TO ENDURE – REKINDLED LOVE

Chapter 9 – Cumberland Island

Living near my grandparents worked for Mother, but she firmly felt that she could only stay in Fairhaven until she found something substantial. She wanted to be independent and self-reliant and not rely upon her parents' and their house for more than was necessary. But she needed a job to be able to care for her children, to pay for rent, and to put food on the table. She could do it. She tried to be resilient, but in the heart of the Depression, she struggled to find suitable work. Every once in a while, an ad appeared in the newspaper for someone to clean a house or care for children, but she was the daughter of a well-respected New Bedford family and needed a respectable job and one that paid an adequate wage. She worked odd jobs for people, but didn't find anything that seemed to fit. She desperately wanted to escape from under her parents' wings and stand on her own two feet.

At thirteen, I became a teenager and adjusted well to the Fairhaven school system. Sarah adapted quickly too. We had shifted around from school to school so much that I found it easier to make friends at this school partially because most of the teachers knew of my grandfather, and many knew my mother. Everyone seemed to like Sarah and me. My education suffered from the change in curriculum from one school to another. I found academics hard, but easily caught up on some subjects, and found myself ahead in other subjects.

Mother on the other hand, could not wait to get out of Fairhaven/New Bedford and see another part of the world. Still, she honored her obligations: financial obligations and the wellbeing of her children. One day after searching to no avail for a decent job, she decided to write a close childhood friend, Lucy Ferguson. She met Lucy at one of her father's social gatherings in New Bedford as a child. They had hit it off.

Lucy's Grandfather, John Howland Ricketson, passed away one year prior to my mother's birth and his family buried him in New Bedford. John shared the same middle name as my mother, Howland. Lucy enjoyed many of the same things as Mother and they thought of themselves more as sisters, even though they were distant cousins. They both liked nice things, but didn't mind hard work. They both valued a flare for fun and enjoyed each other's company. If they had lived in the same town, they may have been best friends. Lucy's family lived in Georgia, spending the winters there. In the summer, they came north to their New England cottage, a remnant of Lucy's Grandfather's estate. That's where my mother and Lucy met.

My mother also liked Lucy because of her name and heritage. Lucy's full name was Lucy Carnegie Ricketson. Decades earlier, John Ricketson married Margaret Coleman Carnegie, and Lucy was their granddaughter. Margaret Carnegie Rickerson was Andrew Carnegie's niece. She inherited part of the Andrew Carnegie industrial empire. At three years old, Lucy moved to Cumberland Island along with many of the other Carnegie family members.

TO ENDURE – REKINDLED LOVE

Thomas Carnegie, Andrew Carnegie's brother and Margaret C. Carnegie's father, established a presence on the island in the 1880s. They wanted a winter retreat. They purchased ninety percent of the island, and, in 1884, built a mansion on that property known as Dungeness. The mansion sported 59 rooms and looked like a Scottish style castle. Pools, a golf course, and 40 other smaller dwellings decked the Mansion.[43] Margaret Carnegie built the local Inn which was finished in 1905 as one of those buildings along with the Farm. Later, other buildings were constructed nearby as houses for their children.

Lucy married Robert Weeks Ferguson and they raised three children: Robert Junior, Oliver, and Maggie (named after her Great Grandmother, Margaret). Maggie was a year younger than me. The boys were a year or two older than I. Robert Weeks Ferguson was a local politician and a state representative.

The local hotel and the farm became owned and operated by Lucy Carnegie Ferguson who inherited both and managed them in a serious fashion.[44]

Lucy was elated when she received the letter out of the blue from my mother. She missed her childhood friend. Lucy immediately wrote back to Mother and asked, "Can you come to Cumberland Island to help me here? The island isn't much, and is a shell of what it used to be, but it

---

[43] After the crash and the Great Depression, the castle and its buildings remained vacant. It ultimately burned to the ground in 1959.
[44] After the depression ended and the economy thrived again, The Plum Orchard was donated to the National Park Service in 1972. To this day, the local Plantation is privately owned that includes an air strip and homes built to house members of the Carnegie family.

is mine to manage."

Mother wrote back and said, "I am available, but my husband and I are divorced, and I have two children. It sounds like the Island can become the adventure of a lifetime for all of us." Mother knew how to express herself well.

Lucy replied to Mother using her childhood nickname, "Kitty, I'd love to have you come down here. You'll love the Island like I love it. Plus, I need a tutor for my kids. You can tutor your children and mine together. We'll work something out."

Lucy's objective and job was to conserve the Island for future generations and possessed the resources needed and could easily afford the visit.

Initially, Mother really hoped Lucy would use her connections to help her obtain a well-paying job in Massachusetts, specifically near or in New Bedford. That did not happen. Even during the depression, well connected people didn't have much to offer. But, when Lucy suggested that my mother could home school her children, Mother jumped at the chance. With Sarah and me in tow, she didn't say anything to my father or even ask, "Aye, Yes or No". She headed to Georgia.

After we arrived at the island, Mother and Lucy sat down and must have talked for over an hour, going over old times and catching up on all the new developments. Mother told Lucy everything. "I just detested staying near my parents. I felt like a drain on them. I really wanted a new start."

Lucy said, "Well Kitty, you have a good opportunity here and I

TO ENDURE – REKINDLED LOVE

hope it meets your satisfaction. You'll have the run of the school. If there is anything you need or want, just let me know."

She tutored two of Lucy's three kids, plus Sarah and me at this enormously big estate on Cumberland Bay. We loved the large island and the estate with lots of room to roam and explore.

We accessed the horses anytime we wanted. We would saddle them up and ride all over the seventeen-mile island. The lovely weather encouraged us to go swimming any-old-time. Storms occurred, but they weren't very serious.

Schools on Cumberland Island were nonexistent, and most of the children from the island went to Fernandina to go to school that would require a boat-ride up a river a few miles. They boarded with relatives or others so they could obtained a proper education. Other children were homeschooled or tutored by a willing adult. So, Mother settled into her position to teach both groups of children to the local hotel. It seemed like a match made in heaven. Mother taught, I cleaned out horse stalls, and my mother and Lucy caught up on all the wonderful and not so wonderful things happening in their lives. We enjoyed the warm weather all year around. We did not miss the weather in the winter in New Bedford, which included dank, dreary, cold and wet days.

Mother felt her children needed to keep a connection with Dad. But Dad had moved across the country to live with Aunty Kay, his other sister and second oldest. He sweated it out in California, trying to get back on his feet. To communicate, Mother expected us to write letters to him weekly the only reasonable way connect. Phones were available on the Island but there was a charge for long distance and it was prohibitively expensive.

Georgia focused us on a new lifestyle with new adventures. I looked forward to the challenge, although Sarah might not have felt the same. She missed her friends in Fairhaven. But both of us "kept that stiff upper lip" and decided we must make the best of it.

Beauty surrounded us on Cumberland Island. The island stretched for 17 miles and was separated from the mainland by the Cumberland Sound, and various rivers that curved from the north tip of the island, around to the wider central portion, and ended at the southern point. We enjoyed being near the beach every day. Sarah and I liked the sun and climate. Despite Lucy's strict demeanor, my mother gave a great deal of freedom to both Ferguson children and to us. We stayed at local hotel in the servants' quarters, but could go where we wanted; we had the run of the place. I enjoyed the outdoors, and it felt like heaven to me.

The two older boys at local hotel did not interact with me at first. Lucy told Oliver to take me around local hotel and the Stafford Plantation. The plantation did not look like what I thought a plantation should look like. Some cotton grew and some vegetables, but there was also a huge pasture for the herd of cows and many horses to graze. Oliver cordially discussed the Island with me, but he clearly wanted to be elsewhere and could not be bothered in becoming my friend. Sarah became friendly with the girl named Maggie.

After a few weeks, the novelty wore off. We settled into a routine on the island. Mother learned the ropes and began reading books and planning classroom activities. She also planned some common activities for all of us to participate, but she taught four grade levels and

TO ENDURE – REKINDLED LOVE

needed to be prepared for our individual instructional needs. First my mother needed to find out what each of her students knew. Once she figured that out, she needed to discover new curriculum for us. It became a monumental task. She persevered, each night talking to Lucy about her children's education. Both Lucy and my mother pieced together a curriculum and let it play out in the classroom. Since Mother needed to focus on her job, which was the Ferguson children's education, Sarah and my individual instruction seemed a bit casual and at times secondary. She required me to study, but I didn't. Sarah did better being tutored by Mother[45].

A small room at local hotel became our classroom. It normally served as a conference room where the Carnegie family met in to discuss matters. Mostly remaining vacant during the day, it made a perfect setting for the classroom. Mother ran class from 8:00 o'clock in the morning until 3:00 o'clock in the afternoon. She made classwork grueling. My education normally consisted of similar instruction to what she taught Oliver and Sarah to what she taught Maggie. It turned out fine, because both of Lucy's children remained a grade level above us, and both Sarah and I enjoyed the challenge. After 3:00 pm Mother released us from school, but my mother worked until about 5:00 pm, planning the next day's lessons. Lucy, being a strict employer, expected a great deal from my mother and the rest of us. Although my mother homeschooled me for a few months, I never really missed out. I viewed it as a good thing. Traditional school programs never questioned my experience for those few months.

---

[45] Later, she went on to Lincoln High School and did well.

Larry Calkins

As for me, my workday began at 3:00 pm. Mother told me to immediately go to the horse stalls. Lucy owned some prize horses. The few months I remained on the Island, I worked hard, caring for the horses with Solomon, the stable man, and cleaning horse stalls. Solomon taught me well. I learned a great deal about horses, horse etiquette, and how to care for them. I liked the horses. Cleaning stalls, however, stunk. Cleaning stalls became a payment for my board and room. I obliged because I did it for my family. For two hours, I helped Solomon care for the horses who reported my progress back to Lucy. During the cleaning of the stalls, I wasn't be very productive. Instead, I daydreamed of adventures I could take around the island, of girls that may trigger my fancy, or of pure fantasies I would dream up. Often Solomon would interrupt me and tell me to get back to work, or to work faster. He expected me to do the work that a teenage boy would do. Half-hearted effort would not be tolerated. I worked with Solomon seven days a week because the horses didn't take a day off, and their stalls needed to be cleaned every day. After work, I went home to find dinner on the table. The evening would be time for my homework.

I also paid my way by doing odd jobs around the place and driving people where they wanted to go. I enjoyed driving all over the place, and I kind of became the chauffeur. When someone wanted to go anywhere, they got me to drive them. The cars were older cars, probably early 1920s. Since Cumberland Island remained privately owned, nobody had any license plates, they just drove. If Mr. Ferguson wanted to go down to the boat, I would drive him down to the boat. If something needed to be fetched, I'd do the fetching. If we needed something being delivered by boat, I'd wait by the dock and bring food or whatever was dropped off back to the Ferguson's big place.

TO ENDURE – REKINDLED LOVE

Mr. Ferguson would find me, "Travis, The Captain is waiting for me, so I can attend my meeting in in Atlanta, and I need a ride to the boat. Also, Lucy tells me she wants you to bring some supplies back when you return. Can you do that for me?"

"Sure, be happy to." I really enjoyed driving those old jalopies.

The people who did all the work around the house were African Americans. They were very respectful. Lucy, a small woman, ran the whole place very efficiently even though she was quite deaf. She had a hearing aid and got along okay. We would talk to her alright but needed to be mindful. Although she did not pay close attention to us kids, she took extraordinary care to pay Mother and us enough, so Mother could go her own way.

The morning and early afternoons on the weekends were mine. I took off to explore the island, sometimes with Sarah and sometimes not. I explored every nook and cranny of the island. I particularly relished in spending time at the beach. Shells and pebbles lay on the vast stretches of sand where I could run and be myself. I spent hours exploring and came back to local hotel tired and happy.

Larry Calkins

TO ENDURE – REKINDLED LOVE

Chapter 10 – Florida

After a few months of working daily, I grew tired of doing stable work. I became more interested in riding horses or driving cars than doing any work, of any kind, including proper schoolwork. My mother was not to blame. She was talented woman, but teaching four grades at once with individualized attention was extremely demanding. I had not become chummy with either Robert or Oliver. I clearly did not perform as well as expected. My mother discussed the situation with Lucy, and they both decided I needed a structured classroom. The only location where I could obtain a decent education nearby became located in Fernandina Beach, Florida. Previously, Lucy sent her children to public schools there. Lucy's relatives in Fernandina fixed me up, boarded me, and provided me with a way to go to school.

The day I left, we drove down to the dock closest to the local hotel and near where we stayed. Sarah teared up. I told Sarah, "We'll see you soon, kid. I'll be back before you know it. Don't worry about me, and take care of Mother."

Sarah said, "Travis don't go. I'm not going to see you for a long time."

Larry Calkins

I responded, "It'll be okay." I turned to Mother and gave her a goodbye kiss then hugged Sarah. Sarah sobbed.

Mother stood stiffly waiving to me, with her other hand in Sarah's, as I walked to the boat where the captain waited for me. There were quick introductions, I hopped aboard, and would not see Mother or Sarah for several months and pushed the thoughts of not seeing my mother or sister for several months out of my mind.

Sarah continued her studies with Mother on the island.

I did not do any significant schoolwork until I got to Fernandina and went to High School. I entered this poor southern public school as a freshman. I had a good teacher, but the setting could have been better. Boarding on my own was not a bad situation for a teenager though.

To get to Fernandina Beach, I took a boat across the Saint Maries River, from the southern portion of Cumberland Island, and up another river called the Amelia River. Fernandina Beach is located a short distance up the Amelia River, in the far northeastern portion of Florida. I spent the remainder of the year there.

The boat ride seemed long. The Captain expertly navigated the rivers that were wide and deep. Along the way, I looked back at the beaches from the river's perspective instead of the perspective of Cumberland Island, and I dreamed of exploring the beaches on the other side of the river. The Captain made sure I was delivered to one of Lucy's relatives, and I took up residence in one of their spare rooms.

Florence Perkins, Lucy's aunt, owned a large house in Fernandina Beach with enough rooms to board relatives and strangers alike. She took me in as a favor to Lucy, but in turn she expected me to do dishes and help out after dinner in the kitchen. Florence, a kind older woman, enjoyed children and raised one grown child of her own. Her husband had just passed, and her son was ill. She spent most of her time caring for him. Another boarder was also a freshman in High School. So, I boarded with this rather supercilious kid. I could not figure out what irritated me about him, except I thought of him as a jerk. He probably thought of me as a jerk too.

Strangely enough, I got a good education in Fernandina. The little town consisted of about twenty-seven hundred people at the very most.

Mrs. Perkins expected me to work, and I accomplished tasks after school and before dinner. After dinner, the boarders' dishes needed to be washed and put away, and I cleaned up the dining and kitchen areas before I did any homework. This did not leave time for many friends except on the weekends. On the weekends, I went to my friends' homes. We pretended we participated in the Great War as soldiers or medics or that we steered mighty boats as captains sailing the rivers and oceans in exploration of treasure. We also spent time exploring the Fernanda Beach area which was covered in trees, and had plenty of places to explore and the beaches to find treasures.

To attend school, I walked from downtown, past an old school building. This schoolhouse was a small deep red brick two-story building used to educate elementary-aged children. If Sarah had not stayed with Mother on Cumberland Island, she may have gone to school there.

Larry Calkins

I continued to walk another a quarter mile further to get to a large open city block where the High School was. Built in 1927, Fernandina High School was two-story light brown brick building with twelve classrooms. It housed the four-year high school students. Now as a teenager and freshman I forged ahead in my new adventure, and one teacher, in particular, provided me excellent instruction. I learned a lot from him and picked up concepts quickly.

Fernandina High School

I easily passed most of my tests, and felt productive during my time there. Although I repeated some topics, I was challenged in others. Some of the materials I studied required prerequisites I didn't have, but I challenged myself to understand what teachers taught, and I quickly grasped the concepts and moved on.

I begged to try out for football at the school. They allowed me to play football, but because I got such a late start on the team, the only position left for me to play happened to be offensive tackle. I loved football, and so it did not bother me. Most linemen weighed much more and were much larger than me, and it sometimes became difficult to get in their way enough to prevent them from tackling the quarterback. I only weighed one-hundred fifty-five pounds, which made it hard to block a two-hundred pounder. My low confidence hampered my determination, and I kind of gave up before I had a chance to succeed. I should have worked harder, because I developed into a strong young man anyway. Although small, I learned to "submarine" under my opponent to knock him off his feet and keep him from getting into the backfield. I was grateful to be on the team, but I did not see a great deal of action on the

TO ENDURE – REKINDLED LOVE

playing field.

Frankly, the Florida experience blurred by, quickly and uneventfully. Free time became a premium between school, football, working at the Perkins, and homework. At the Perkins most of the time; unlike on Cumberland Island, the weekends were not mine. Mrs. Perkins expected me to help out around the house, gardening, cleaning house, or fixing broken items that needed repair. But I did not have a mentor here, so I either figured it out myself or left it for someone else to do. Mother taught me how to clean house, a bit about gardening, but I struggled to fix broken items.

I had been separated from Mother, Sarah for nearly three quarters of a year while I stayed in Florida. I finally somewhat accepted my parent's separation. I still missed Dad terribly. I hurled myself into my new environment, mostly alone, and dreamed of having Dad back in my life. As a young teenager, I found it hard to accept my predicament, but I could do nothing about it. My life remained regulated. I wrote my father about once every week or two, but I yearned for the sound of his voice. Still, Fernandina remained a good experience for me.

Larry Calkins

TO ENDURE – REKINDLED LOVE

Chapter 11 – Moses Brown

Mother and Sarah stayed in Georgia, and I in Florida nearly a year. It became an excellent experience for us. After our experience, Mother decided she wanted to return to New England. She would not say it, but I think she tired of teaching Lucy's children. She gave it a good try, but did not realize how tough it would be until she worked at it for several months. After a little over a year homeschooling Lucy's children and Sarah, she realized she needed to find something more significant, something fulfilling. She returned to Fairhaven in early June 1938.

While Mother and Sarah lived in Georgia and I in Fernandina, we got news that my grandfather, Edwin, became very sick. I believe it became a significant reason for Mother to return to Fairhaven. She wanted to be there for her mother as her mother had previously cared for her. When we arrived, right after school finished for the year, my grandfather was unable to greet us because he slept most of the time. Mother sat by his bed and held his hand. Later that month, he passed away. I had mixed feelings. I was sad about the situation and felt sorry for Mother and Grandmother, but was also ambivalent because the old man would not be around to torment my father any longer.

Sarah and I returned to school in Fairhaven in the fall of 1938. We completed nearly another year of schooling at Fairhaven. I did pretty well, getting As and Bs. However, I could focus better on school being in Fernandina. I had distractions in Fairhaven. Mother helped my Grandmother tie up loose ends left by my grandfather's departure. I lived a melancholy existence for the next year, recognizing that Mother and Grandmother were regrouping their lives, trying to make the best of things.

Grandmother knew the headmaster of Moses Brown in Providence, Rhode Island. She had attended Lincoln when a child, as had Mother. Lincoln and Moses Brown were associated; Lincoln educated the girls; and Moses Brown educated the boys. Grandmother learned of a job being a matron of one of the boy's dormitories. Mother had taught boys that age at Lucy's house and knew something of classroom decorum. So Grandmother reasoned that if Mother could handle me, she could handle any boy at Moses Brown. Mother applied for the job and, to our amazement, got it. It helped that my mother attended Lincoln School as a young lady, which was run by the same people, and her brother attended Moses Brown in prior years. The schools liked returning family members. It stretched Mother, but she learned fast.

Moses Brown offered education as a prestigious college preparatory school in New England. The school is operated based on Quaker values that every person matters. It drew students from all over the eastern seaboard, but primarily from New England. Many of the students went on to Ivy League colleges and made names for themselves.

When Moses Brown began the school in 1904, it started as a coed school. In 1926, Moses Brown became an all-boys school to reflect the period. Because Quakers believe in gender equality, they were serious about educating girls too. Lincoln School began in 1884, started

TO ENDURE – REKINDLED LOVE

by Mrs. William Ames to help educate her daughter. In 1888, it took on the name of John Larkin Lincoln, who educated students at Brown University with a strong interest in educating girls and young women. In 1924, it became a Quaker School. Consequently, in 1926, when Moses Brown became an all-boys school, the Quakers already operated Lincoln School, so it complemented nicely with their educational goals in the New England area.

The best part of Mother obtaining the matron job at Moses Brown was that her children attended their respective schools tuition free. This pleased both my mother and grandmother as Sarah was just entering high school.

When applying for entrance to Moses Brown, Mother had to smooth talk the administration because I did not have the prerequisites. She likely said, "Look, Travis is perfectly smart, he can handle all this. Let's just put him in as a junior and see how he does." She typically had a way with people and saw to it that they admitted me as a junior. So, I attended Moses Brown, and Sarah attended Lincoln. It was a tough eye-opening experience for me. Mother recognized the difficulty I had in school, but I survived. I eventually received my certificate from Moses Brown School, thanks to Mother's ability to get people to see things her way.

I distinctly remember how hard my lessons were at Moses Brown as most of my schoolwork before came relatively easy. As a private school, Moses Brown developed curriculum way ahead of anything I had previously learned. I became determined to learn as much as I could as quickly as I could. I really struggled and remained behind, scraping by with Cs and Ds. The strict teachers at Moses Brown challenged me every step of the way beyond my capability. I had no room for slacking, and I didn't. I needed to study and study hard. The teachers seemed sympathetic to my circumstances, but they also needed to meet their school requirements. Still, somehow, I met enough of their expectations.

One teacher said to me, "Travis I understand your situation and you have not had the opportunity many of these students have had. You will be struggling. But, that's okay. Keep trying. You may surprise yourself." The teacher continued to reassure me, "I can't treat you any differently than I would other students on campus. I've talked to your mother. She remains confident in your abilities, and so am I. You hang in there, and you'll get through it."

My time at Moses Brown thoroughly prepared me for college. I was grateful for that opportunity to learn and grateful for the training I received from these rigorous and high expectations. It taught me to focus and push to do as well as I could. Because of my lower grades, I looked toward the bottom of the student-academic-achievement roster to find my name. When it came to discuss my future educational possibilities, none of us were very optimistic. Still, both the school and I persevered must have done something right because I kept the goal of going to college alive.

Moses Brown Prep School

I tried to be independent, but Mother would always find me after several days to check up on me. She did the same for Sarah.

Ever since a young age, I loved playing football. From what my

TO ENDURE – REKINDLED LOVE

uncles taught me to what I learned on the field in Florida, I was not going to give it up. So, I decided to try out for the Moses Brown football team. I expected fun, dreamed of being a good player, but also expected a challenge. I got all of it. As a scrappy teenager who quickly executed his moves, I did not mind blocking, or at least standing in the way of guys much larger than me. This proved helpful on the field. I became a pulling guard, one who lined up on offense on the left side and swept right pulling away from my position, running into the backfield to block the first opponent I saw, often a massive right tight end. If I succeeded, the running back had a clear shot for at least five to ten yards. I became pretty effective at that position, and Moses Brown played me often to make that play several times every game. I felt an increase in my self-esteem being part of a team with that kind of success.

For two years I played this position and liked it just strengthened my resolve. Pep rallies, though, were especially gratifying because they jazzed the team up and got our adrenaline going, knowing we needed to perform up to the expectations of the crowds. It felt good to stand as a team and receive accolades from our classmates.

I also tried out for wrestling. I excelled at this sport because I wrestled by weight class. So, I wrestled kids my own size.

I tried my hand at track as well. I liked long distance running. It became a test of endurance and skill. I did not need to be an extremely fast runner, although I liked to see how fast I could run. The coach pulled me aside before a meet started and said, "Travis, I have a strategy for you. You want our school to win, right?"

I responded, "Certainly."

The coach continued, "Good. Then what I want you to do when the starting gun goes off is to begin with a sprint. I want you to get ahead of the pack of runners the best you can. You are a good runner and can stay ahead of them. Once you have the other team trying to catch you, you can slow down about half to three quarters the way through and let our other strong runners pass you. I want to tire out the other team. You are the decoy."

I did not mind, although the word decoy threw me for a while. I knew we had some strong long-distance runners, and they had an edge knowing I would be tiring out the other team. If I succeeded, I could be the team hero—or so I told myself.

As a college preparatory school, each student was expected to move on to a higher institution of learning. As Moses Brown trained students academically, and as much as I struggled to get decent grades, the experience, on the whole, toughened my psyche and strengthened my soul. It prepared me for what lay ahead, which included the military and college. I tried, my efforts were enough, and I learned to never give up.

TO ENDURE – REKINDLED LOVE

Chapter 12 – California

I finally finished all my classes, retook classes I failed, and graduated from Moses Brown. While my grades were not stellar, I look back on the whole experience with appreciation and a little fondness. I am thankful mainly for what I accomplished and the rigor I was able to obtain. I figured I did not have many choices but to work in 1941. The school advised me to find some sort of employment either through the newly formed CCC (Civilian Conservation Corps) or a war-related job, such as producing airplanes in California.

Before I graduated, the United States began a military buildup, anticipating war. Now, upon graduation, the military buildup continued. The United States was neutral at the time, but we were also manufacturing war machinery. My family, and the rest of the United States, saw Germany takeover of most of Europe, and we became appalled at the ability of one country to amass such an empire in such a short amount of time. The Asian Pacific war also heated up as Japan also began to take over different regions, attempting to build their influence.

World War II raged elsewhere when I graduated. Japan already had been at war with China since 1937. In 1939, Nazi Germany invaded Poland. In September 1940, Germany, Italy, and Japan entered into a Tripartite Pact to form the Axis.[46]

Subsequently, France and the United Kingdom declared war on Germany.[47] By 1941, Germany controlled much of Europe. In June 1941, Germany, Italy and Romania launched an attack against the Soviets.

In July, Japan sent troops into southern Indonesia threatening British and Dutch possessions in that area.[48] In November 1941, Japan failed to come to agreement with the United States over a nonaggression pact with all pacific neighbors. Japan considered the failure to reach an agreement and an oil embargo as an act of war.

On December 7, Japan attacked Pearl Harbor, the Philippines and British holdings in Thailand, Malaya, and Hong Kong. These attacks caused the United States, the United Kingdom, China and Australia to declare war on Japan.

---

[46] The Pact stated that if country not at war attacked any of the three countries, it would be considered an attack on all the countries. Other countries were added later to the Pact. In 1939, the US revoked its trade treaty with Japan beginning with an aviation gasoline ban in 1940. China had effectively blocked supply routes. Japan began to feel economic pressures and the war between Japan and China stalemated.

[47] Germany invaded Denmark and Norway in the Spring of 1940 to protect iron ore shipments from Sweden to Germany. Once secured, Hitler planned an offensive in France. First Paris and then all of France fell to Germany's control in June.

[48] Western Countries reacted to this invasion with an oil embargo. In early 1941, the United States and Japan had been in negotiations to try to help end the war in China. Roosevelt reinforced troops in the Philippines, a US protectorate, warning Japan that the US would react if there were attacks on any neighboring countries. Frustrated by all the sanctions, Japan started building for war.

TO ENDURE – REKINDLED LOVE

This buildup of tension in 1941 made for a robust airplane industry. Many of the manufacturers of airplanes were in California. More and more orders of military planes came in from the United Kingdom, the U.S. Government, and others.

The events leading up to the US involvement to World War II, stimulated a corresponding buildup in war related materials, just in case we entered the war. California included many airplane manufacturing jobs. I saw it as a way to land a job there and as the primary reason I wanted to go to California.

I wrote Dad in Los Angles after I graduated from Moses Brown. I told him I wanted to visit him in California. I did not have any money to go to college, nor could my mother help me through college, like she did through Moses Brown, so I decided to go to work. I talked Malcolm, another classmate, into going to California with me, where we could both take advantage of the abundance of good jobs.

Dad still lived with his sister (Aunt Kay) in California. The last time I'd seen Aunt Kay, was when she'd come to see my family in Massachusetts when I was about five years old. She had no clue what I looked like. Kay, a lovely person, freely accepted people and situations. She was willing to open her heart to the son of her brother, whom she adored. Mother did not get along with Kay or Lucile, but it didn't matter.

I just announced, "Mother, I am going to California. I plan to stay with Dad and try to get a job at an aerospace company that's hiring. Malcomb wants to go with me."

She was a nut and sometimes surprised me with her responses. She had an interesting way of looking at it. I never really thought she would say yes. Instead, she responded, "Why yes. I think you ought to do that. ...Wonderful."

So, I said, "Okay then, well, we're going." Mother wished me luck and waved goodbye. I had some money in the bank, I took it out, and Malcolm and I went off together to purchase one-way tickets to California.

I knew that Aunty Kay lived somewhere in Southern California. I had missed the warm weather of Georgia and Florida and figured California would be just right. I had little to lose. Malcolm and I took a bus to Southern California.

When I arrived in California, I was shocked by how massive the Los Angeles area was. I had no idea where to look for Aunty Kay. I kept asking people where to find her house. Finally, we found it.

I appeared at the front door, knocked, and when it opened, I said, "Hello Aunty Kay."

She asked, "Who are you?"

I replied, "I'm your nephew, and this is my friend Malcomb."

Aunty Kay did not recognize me at first. Then she could not believe her eyes or ears, being stunned I had come all the way to California. She welcomed me with open arms and even had a room for us to stay in. I understood her confusion when she saw a seventeen year old boy show up at her door step unannounced.

When my father arrived home that evening, he was as shocked as Aunty Kay had been upon seeing me. He knew I was thinking about coming because of the last letter I wrote him, but I never told him I had made a decision or, more importantly, that I was on my way. I just showed up.

I told him "Dad, Malcomb and I are going to stay out here and get jobs."

Aunt Kay kept fussing over me until I felt right at home. I was relieved we had completed the trip and thrilled that they were excited to see us

Dad, Aunt Kay, Malcolm, and I talked late into the night. Dad and Aunt Kay wanted to hear everything about our adventures traveling across the country and my experiences as a teenager. I told them of my experiences in Georgia, and how I went to Florida to board and go to school there. I told Dad about playing football. Aunt Kay curiously asked about Moses Brown. I explained my struggle to get good grades and that football had allowed me to escape academic life. She told me how, despite my poor performance academically, she felt a degree from Moses Brown would be valuable for employment, or even college. Aunt Kay also explained the layout of Los Angeles and where we'd find the aerospace industry.

The next day, Malcolm and I went searching for a job. I had little experience, but I had drive and ambition, and I figured that should count for something. I wanted to go to several industrial operations, starting in Burbank, CA. I walked into one aerospace company and they immediately hired me. As long as I passed some rudimentary tests, I could start work. With a snap of the fingers, I had a job. I was elated at my good fortune and shared details with Dad and Aunt Kay. I was determined to keep this first real job from slipping through my fingers. Again, we were thrilled when Malcolm got a similar job. The bosses seemed to like us both.

I worked at an aircraft manufacturing facility in Burbank. Some days I still find it hard to believe that I just went in, applied, and they hired me—just like that. Being barely an eighteen-year-old kid, they did not have to pay me anything, because I would work for peanuts. They needed people like crazy as the war still loomed on the horizon. I worked hard for the company that year, enjoyed it very much and made a fair amount of money for myself.

I approached my dad, "Malcolm and I have good jobs now at our company and I am going to find a place to board nearby work."

He said, "Oh, I think that's wonderful." He said "How would you feel about me living with you? I think it's time for me to get back out on my own."

Malcolm and I were surprised but thought it would work well, saving us all money and we could also share household duties.

The arrangement worked out extremely well. Dad had recovered from his nervous breakdown and began to regain his self-respect. He worked for one aerospace company and I worked for another. We all worked, and shared work stories, but also had fun.

Dad, Malcolm and I found our apartment in the Glenwood district in Glendale, a city adjacent to Burbank and near the aerospace company. A month later Malcolm found his own apartment. Glenwood worked well for us. Dad and I enjoyed each other's company. He told me stories about the good old days, and I expressed my dreams of the adventures I wanted to undertake.

At the company, they started me off working as a riveter on B-17 aircraft. England liked the B-17, and I worked on a shipment of those aircraft. Later that summer, I switched to a B-24 aircraft manufacturing line, also set for distribution in England.

I did not realize at the time how important the B-24s would become. In 1943, they were known as the Great Liberator for Europe. They were a four engine, 56,000 pound goliath that conducted a raid on Gotha, Germany, where major aircraft production occurred. The raid devastated the German aircraft production due to the precision bombing by the B-24s.

I continued to help manufacture these aircraft through Operation Camouflage. In the wake of the December 7, 1941 Japanese attack on Pearl Harbor, the government ordered every aircraft that could fly to be in the air. Some flew west to protect the West Coast. Many were simply sent airborne to provide a sense of security for the nation. The officials at the company I worked for met at the manufacturing plant in Burbank to decide how best to ramp up production and provide security to protect the production.

Col. Ohmer, stationed at March Field, seventy miles away, had a significant mission to disguise the Burbank aircraft production facility as another suburb in Los Angles. He recruited painters, artists, and set designers from nearby movie production facilities. Painters painted the airfields and parking lots green and lined them with plants to make them look like alfalfa fields instead. Ohmer covered the main facility in chicken wire, netting, and canvas and painted to look like the surrounding fields. An elaborate system of underground walkways was constructed to allow freedom of movement across the plant. Contractors constructed bomb shelters for employees. Soldiers placed huge anti-aircraft guns in strategic locations around the facility.[49]

I was thrown in the middle of quite a theatrical production, yet still had an important job to do. Others explained that all anyone could see from the air was one California suburb after another. Tensions were high at this time as we found ourselves in the middle of a build up to war, but we felt as secure as one could feel. Plus, every night, I could go back to my apartment and have a good feeling about what I accomplished.

One day, I took Dad to work with me and showed him the vast camouflaged landscape of the Burbank Plant. He could not believe his eyes.

I continued to go to Aunty Kay's house on most Sundays for dinner. She always fixed a good meal with Nancy, her daughter, my cousin a little older than me. Nancy and I became good friends. We would horse around. She attended the University of California, Los Angles, UCLA, and that started me thinking about higher education.

Nancy prodded, "Travis, you ought to go to college. I think UCLA is a good choice for you. What do you think?"

I responded, "Well, I've heard good things about that school." I

---

[49] "Operation Camouflage: Hiding An Entire Aircraft Plant Under a Fake Subdivision" https://interestingengineering.com/operation-camouflage-hiding-aircraft-plant-under-fake-subdivision

TO ENDURE – REKINDLED LOVE

did not know if I could get in. "Maybe I'll try and see what happens."

I continued to support the war effort by working at the Burbank plant and wrote Mother about the great time Dad and I were having together. I would laugh as I wrote the letters, embellishing them a little to entice Mother come to California. I explained how Dad and I laughed and carried on, running all over Los Angles in the warm California sun.

When, Mother received my letters, she began to romanticize about California and thought of days filled with sunshine sounded wonderful. She finally had enough and wrote back, "I'm coming out! You can't have all the fun."

Mother remained a kid at heart who was up for a new adventure and wanted to be in the action with Dad and me. With two difficult people passing away, her father and mother-in-law, she felt much less tied down. She talked to her mother and explained why she wanted to go to California—not that it mattered, she planned to go anyway.

It did not take much to convince Mother that she needed a change from New England. Sunny California seemed like an ideal place, especially in the winter, and she could get a job and bloom like Dad and I had. With Sarah grown and graduating in the spring and my mother could bring Sarah to California too. Mother could now dream of living in paradise. California seemed like the land of make believe, a land of fairy tales and princesses and princes, and she could once again "make believe."

Strangely, the family unexpectedly reunited in Los Angeles, California in 1942. Mother made the arrangements for Sarah and herself to join us in California. When Mother arrived, she became excited and full of fun. She went out on the town with Dad and me, and we enjoyed our time as a family again.

Mother and Dad clicked like old times. Mother had always felt a strong responsibility to her family that included my dad. She left Dad at the insistence of her parents during a very difficult time in the economy and in their marriage. She always had loved him, even when they were separated. She never considered remarrying and did not feel comfortable being dependent upon a man again. She planned to continue to be gainfully employed so she could remain an independent woman. But, she also felt a loyalty and dedication to the original bonds of matrimony from twenty years earlier. That never went away.

Dad felt similarly. He never really loved anyone the way he loved my mother. The ember in his soul that nearly died because of their separation, ignited once again. Dad's self-esteem shot up like a rocket. His former sadness gave away to joy. The sparkle that I had seen as a young boy of six or seven returned to his eyes. Dad became more talkative and lively and more energetic, finding things around the apartment to do. He started painting and etching dogs, people, buildings, and boats again.

They shoved the cold and dreary winter days of New England behind both of them. I could see the excitement and love that Dad once had for Mother on his face, and he acted forty years old again. It seemed like my parents were still married, but better. Mother even had that impish way about her as she teased my father. Much of the time they would be in their own world, and my presence did not really matter. I happily accepted their reignited love, and ventured out on my own.

TO ENDURE – REKINDLED LOVE

Mother and Dad moved back in together about the time I decided to go to college at University of California Los Angles (UCLA) because I had saved a little money working at the aerospace company. Nancy agreed to show me the ropes, although I really did not need her to and we rarely saw each other. But I felt comfort knowing she attended the school, and I could call on her if needed. I went to UCLA for part of a year, then got drafted.

In 1943, they drafted me into the Army at the age of nineteen. I served in the US Army during World War II. At that time, draftees were allowed to apply for pilot training in the Army Air Corps. I saw a sign on the bulletin board in the mess hall one day, announcing the pilot training and asking for volunteers. I began to wonder if this would be a good vocation. A short time later, I stood in a lineup and the sergeant came in and asked a question about those interest in the pilot training.

He said, "Those not interested in Pilot Training, take one step back."

I was still thinking about the possibility, when I realized I was only one of a handful of recruits that did not take the step back. I became a pilot by default. I never regretted it.

Travis Calkins
WWII pilot trainee

The Army Air Corps continued to be a part of the Army[50] at that time and relatively new. Not many soldiers considered this new division. I figured if I volunteered, it would

---

[50] The Army Air Corps eventually became the United States Air Force.

create less of a chance I could get shot at if we were dragged into the war. The risky decision had its positive points, and in my youth, I continually looked for new prospects.

As reality set in, I found many of the pilots did not return. They were either shot down, made a fatal mistake, or were just plain unlucky.[51] I thought I might secure a better place in life once the war ended, and, at that point, could even be a hero.

As part of the initial training, the Army Air Corps sent us cadets to Washington State College in Pullman, Washington, to improve our intellectual powers. The Air Corps conducted rigorous lectures, along with physical and mock flying exercises at the school.

After the lectures and exercises were completed, I returned to Santa Anna, California, in February of 1944, to begin the flight instruction to become a Flight Officer. I started out flying the PT-22 training aircraft, a military version of the civilian Ryan ST-3. The Army Air Corp ordered this plane, also called "the Recruit," in large numbers to assist in training pilots during the buildup before the war.

Similarly, I began learning on the BT-13 aircraft, another basic training aircraft. Once mastering these planes, I graduated to the AT-17 and IC-78 aircraft which were twin engine aircraft that bridged the gap between single engine trainers and twin engine combat aircraft.

---

[51] I became one of the lucky ones. I always wanted to fly, and now I took advantage of the opportunity.

TO ENDURE – REKINDLED LOVE

As I trained as a pilot during the first part of 1944, I sent letters back and forth to my sister Sarah. I shared what I was learning and my dreams of becoming an official pilot with her.

Dear Sarah,

Sorry to hear you're under the weather – If it's anything like the weather around here you must be in a bad way. There hasn't been a clear day at this field since they built the place – Come to think of it, I can't figure out why they did build it. But – we fly anyway. Why it got so cold up there the other day that my instructor's words froze as they came though the gosports and I kept hearing them all the way down. Far-fetched wasn't it?

Say, you should have been here the other night when the upper class had their graduating banquet. It really was a kick. I wasn't supposed to go, but after the dinner was over, I sneaked in and listened to the shit my roommates put on as a take-off on their officers. As a final gesture of their regard they presented the three tactical officers with a fur-lined bedpan saying that they hoped the three of them could get together on it. On the bottom was painted "the class of 44E looks up to you."

Ah yes, I wish I were going with the boys. I'm afraid this place won't be worth living in after they're gone. Day before yesterday, I took a check flight and when I came down the instructor said – "well let's call that your twenty hour check," so I passed the first hurdle.

Now, there are two more here at primary. I have about thirty hours now.

Have you guys found a place to live yet? From what I hear gas is going to be so hard to get they're thinking of cutting out "A" coupons entirely. You'd better move someplace near your work. Why don't you get a defense house? Gotta Go.

Love Travis

My Jan. 1943 letter to my sister, Sarah

Larry Calkins

By June 27, 1944, I passed all my training aircraft. Once I mastered the training planes, I moved directly into the B-26 aircraft. This medium sized twin engine bomber became a serious weapon of war in both the Pacific and European theaters of war. Initially, the B-26 was called the widow-maker, because early versions of the plane were operated by inexperienced pilots and the relatively short wing-span required a fast landing. Several accidents had occurred. By 1944, though, most of the problems were resolved, and pilots of the B-26 had contained its combat losses to the lowest of any U.S. aircraft during the war.

***

The hype of the war and my parent's rekindled love had emotions surging through the veins of our family. My father and mother decided to get remarried. They renewed their marriage in a simple ceremony performed by a justice of the peace in Los Angles. Even though it was somewhat of a quiet a reunion, I still felt somewhat responsible for this wonderful event.

My parents finally took my advice and listened to Sarah's prompting and moved into some defense housing. The rent was cheap, and they liked it. The location continued to be close to the Museum of Art and central to most places in Los Angles. Their physical address was located on South Ogden Drive, Los Angeles, CA. I used this address as my permanent address while I remained deployed in the Army.

Mother secured a job at Bullocks, a department store, selling ladies undergarments.

Dad now considered himself an industrial engineer and continued to work at another aerospace industry. He also advised some

TO ENDURE – REKINDLED LOVE

investment clients in Los Angeles and purchased some securities of his own. Sarah went to work for one of the airlines.

Dad and Mother's marriage seemed to blossom. When my mother came to California, it seemed to give her a new lease on life, and she seemed happy. Dad's joyful personality returned.

Before being deployed to Europe, the Air Corps sent me for a short period to Kerns Field, and then to Hill Airforce Base, just south of Ogden, Utah, for additional pilot training. On August 10, 1944, the Army Air Corps, now referred to as the Army Air Forces (AAF), required me learn to fly the B-26 as I prepared to meet other forces already stationed in London England.

At Hill Airforce Base, I met Billie Jeanne McCarty, hanging out near the base. I fell in love with her right off the bat. Her Mormon religion did not matter to me. Her beauty and personality intrigued me, and I was smitten by her. She and I had spent time together after flight school, and found as much time as was possible before I left for the European Theater deployment. We talked about marriage, and I reminded her I only had limited time in Utah. I expressed my worry about war and what may happen. I, then, asked her to marry me and we became engaged. We decided to wait until I returned from Europe, delaying our wedding plans. I wrote her throughout the war when I could, and she wrote back sustaining my resolve to get home in one piece.

In September, I deployed to London, and Billie Jeanne went to California to stay with my parents. She planned to wait in California for the war to end and then we could reunite. Billie Jeanne found it difficult to live with my parents as I fought in the war. In her defense, she barely knew me, let alone my parents. She decided to move back to Utah. My work remained paramount to my success in the Army Air Forces (AAF) and following through with the war effort was important to me.

In September, the army assigned me to the Ninth Command, the 386th group, and the 553rd squadron, and I prepared to leave for London. The AAF assigned me the role of co-pilot, pairing me with a more experienced pilot on our bombing missions.

When the AAF sent me to the European Theater of Operations (ETO), beginning in September 1944, I logged 33 hours as a co-pilot and four hours as a pilot on the B-26 in the bombardier group. I flew daily missions based out of England. As a flight officer with the AAF, I spent one and a half years in France and England. During the first part of that period, I co-piloted B-26s for seven of those months. Our crew conducted three major missions with the bomb group north of Paris. Our missions required us to bomb enemy supply routes and support facilities.

When I flew the B-26s as a co-pilot, we were usually on a mission, flying in formation, being escorted by smaller P-38s or P-47s. The smaller planes' role assured the large bombers made it to their targets, and the smaller planes scrambled to search out the enemy along the way. The P-38 and P-47 fighters' engaged any German aircraft that showed up, shooting them down. They flew anywhere from 25,000 to 40,000 feet in altitude, conducting S-turns over the bombers to keep enemy fighters away. They would get into big, twisting, turning dogfights with the German Aircraft. But if they were not present, our large B-26 bombers would have been sitting ducks for the Germans, and we would have lost many more of the bombers.

TO ENDURE – REKINDLED LOVE

The Germans, being smart, simply stayed high above our formations, then would dive down in slashing attacks, and zoom back up to where we could not get them. Our large aircraft could only continue on. We hoped the P-38s and P-47s did their job and scared off the German attackers.

The German airmen remained a skilled and formidable foe. Most of them had developed more experience. Many had seen a couple of years or more of combat, where allied forces just had a few months of training. We lost many pilots and aircraft because most of our commanding officers did not have any more experience than we did. I appreciated those that escorted the bombers because I knew we could not have done our job without them. Our plane was simply too big to turn to participate in a dogfight. We focused on our mission, delivering the bombs to the appropriate target. When we got close to the target, we often were met by antiaircraft fire or "flak." We needed to fly through this heavy anti-aircraft fire to deliver the bombs to the targets. This often proved to be the biggest threat. Surprisingly, more often than not, we succeeded in our quests.

Enemy fire was not the only problem. We lost many aircraft due to the weather and poor training. I felt fortunate to receive the training I did and fly with good pilots that knew what they were doing. Even with the most seasoned pilots, weather often caused delays or cancellations of missions. Still, we needed to be able to take off on instruments and land accordingly. I flew through the fog and rain of England into Europe, where better visibility opened up. We always flew in formation, and, during these weather conditions, I was regularly worried about running into one of our own aircraft, more than about running into enemy aircraft.

We typically carried 100 to 500 pound bombs. Sometimes, we carried parachute fragmentation bombs, or parafrags. We dropped them on lightly armored targets. We also had several 50-caliber machine guns depending upon the aircraft model. Some had two or more on each side, just below the cockpit. Also, machine guns located in the top turret and in the tail could be used. When we dropped the bombs, we usually stayed down low until we heard the bombs explode and felt the concussion. Flying so low, we became particularly vulnerable and sustained numerous hits from small arms and antiaircraft fire.

I stayed with the bombardier group until reassigned March 19, 1945 to the 31st transport group and the 314th transport squadron in the European Theater. This next assignment committed me to flying troops and cargo in a C-47 aircraft out of Oxford England on a daily basis.

Travis Calkins, WWII pilot

I flew a C-47, a cargo aircraft, to ferry daily supplies, ammo, and troops to the front lines of the war and bring wounded home. This time, I not only flew 224 hours as a co-pilot, but piloted my own planes for 229 hours. I flew 5 days per week, over the course of ten months. Often, I picked up wounded on the front lines or from a single mat field about 20 miles north of Paris to fly them for care in hospitals near Oxford, England. I avoided catastrophe several times.

Some of the pilots came back with stories of bravery and disaster. I told my share. In 1945, as the front lines moved ever closer to

TO ENDURE – REKINDLED LOVE

Berlin, I flew supplies day after day and knew the terrain pretty well. One day, a co-pilot and the plane's engineer accompanied me in our C-47. We had flown to our destination once before. We spotted the dirt field from some distance away and circled quickly, hardly giving the field a second glance. Easing back on the throttle to land, I looked up, and to my horror, saw that the original runway I planned to land the plane on was marred by a large bomb crater in the middle. To assure the problem would be noticed, someone parked a steamroller between us and the crater. At about a 15-degree angle to the steamroller were faint tracks where other C-47's had made a new runway avoiding the crater. But by this time, we were in imminent danger; I could not to pull up and it was too late not to land. To avoid the mishap, I skidded the large plane sideways to change direction. I nearly stalled the plane while easing the plane along barely a few feet off the ground to avoid crashing. But I knew we were blessed with help from some greater power as we bounced down the turf past the steamroller and crater and came to a stop. I landed the plane safely, but not without difficulty coming within inches of a steam roller and a huge crater what could have spelled disaster. We made it, landing without incident. Thankfully, we avoided any destructive alternative. What a harrowing experience! When we got out, we hid our fears with humor and never spoke of that incident again.[52]

I piloted C-47 transports back and forth. It was a lonely job, in a way. Unlike the bombing missions, we flew unprotected and often took some fire from the enemy. We handled an important task because we not

---

[52] Years later, I felt I missed an opportunity to share some humanity with my co-workers and discuss the fears we had. After the war, I never had the opportunity to see or spoke to those gentlemen again.

only shuttled rations to frontline troops, but also carried drums of aviation gasoline. It became vital to the war effort for those on the frontlines. On our return trips, we conducted an equally important mission: evacuating the sick and wounded.

One day, toward the end of the war, after I'd delivered my supplies to the front, I picked up a few wounded soldiers for transport back to England. Then from out of nowhere, a German attack aircraft pursued us. I figured he would eventually shoot us down. The aircraft approached me quickly. I could not tell at the time what type of aircraft it happened to be, but we clearly observed a German swastika on the tail. It may have been a Me-262 but I couldn't be sure. I knew the Messerschmidtt Me-262, a German fighter, could be faster and more heavily armed than any of the allied planes. It gave both the P-38 and P-47s a run for their money. Of course, without an escort, I had no way to fight back. The German attack aircraft swooped down in a slant from the sky and began tailing me. I saw the enemy planes make this type of move when I flew in the Bombardier Group as they attacked our fighter pilots. Then, just as abruptly as he appeared, he disappeared. I speculated he got low on fuel because the German aircraft did not have an extended range or could not fly far without refueling. He needed to conserve fuel and must have decided he could not chase me. Additionally, he could have seen our transport headed back to England and determined I was not much of a threat.

During this time in the war, Hitler had ordered his infantry and all civilians to pursue any Allied pilot that was shot down and immediately shoot him on sight. The German people began to do this. I felt very lucky the German pilot turned around because a longer pursuit

TO ENDURE – REKINDLED LOVE

may have ended in a different story.

On April 30, 1945, Adolph Hitler killed himself, and the war ended on September 2, 1945. After the war ended, I flew in and out of Germany, transporting supplies and people until the middle of 1946.

On July 4, 1946, I returned home from the European Front and left the war behind. Mother had not seen me for over two years and had many anxious moments wondering if she would ever see me again. When I returned, I walked in on her and Dad unexpectedly. Surprised, she gave a whoop, a holler, and then gave me a big hug. She grabbed me by one hand and Dad by the other and whirled us around the room, still whooping it up, laughing and crying at the same time.

Larry Calkins

TO ENDURE – REKINDLED LOVE

Chapter 13 – After the War

Dad and Mother remained relatively happy together. I noticed that the flames of the second honeymoon period died down. My parents acted like they had lived together for all these years. The hardships were over and the dire circumstances had disappeared. Still, hurdles remained, but life looked much better when they were together.

After the war, Sarah married Will Palmer, a career Army officer.[53]

I was glad to be home and have Mother and Dad dote on me. Mother and Father purchased a nice home on W 59th Street in Los Angles. The home, a single level ranch style house with tile roof and stucco siding, looked like many similar California houses.

W 59th St .Los Angles

---

[53] She traveled all over the world with her husband and three children. She spent significant time in Saigon and another period of time in Hawaii. She and Will retired in Dallas Texas.

Larry Calkins

In July 1946, I raced to Utah to see Billie Jeanne and we began to make plans for our marriage. I wanted to enjoy being married as soon as I could. Billie Jeanne and I started to arrange our wedding. I told her I had to go back to England to the University of Bristol but I would return on September 5th.

I returned to England briefly to spend a couple of months as a student at the University of Bristol. On September 4, 1946—forty-two months and over a thousand hours of flying time after the Army drafted me—I was discharged with an honorable discharge as a Flight Officer. I remained in the service, but became a Reserve Officer, beginning as a Second Lieutenant. I immediately flew home to begin my new life.

On September 16, 1946, Billie Jeanne and I were married. My parents came up to Utah to be with us. We rented a place on E Third Street in Salt Lake City, Utah. Unfortunately, it was obvious after living together for just a few months the marriage was not going to work. She asked me for an annulment. I took it in stride, even though it shook me because it happened so soon. Billie Jeanne had met another man and wanted to marry him. We divorced on March 12, 1947.

I, then, announced I would apply for the GI Bill and go back to college, letting the Army pay for my college.

While back home in 1947 in Los Angeles, I began to serve again in the Reserve in Long Beach, CA. I wrote my grandmother, encouraging her to move to California to be with us. She took a while to respond, but she answered with a very nice letter, stating she had already found a place to live in a retirement home. She appreciated my letter but had made up her mind. She kindly explained why she thought this would be

TO ENDURE – REKINDLED LOVE

the best idea. In 1949, my grandmother, Emma, passed away.

When I first entered the U.S. Army, as part of the initial training, the Air Corps sent us cadets to Washington State College (WSC)[54] in Pullman Washington. They housed me in Ferry Hall where we amused ourselves by bothering the local coeds. I remember one pretty coed, a girl named Eva, who worked at the library and attracted my attention. She provided me a great incentive to improve my reading habits.

After the war ended, I returned to WSC as a GI student since WSC readily accepted veterans, and it did not matter too much what grade point average you previously earned. I looked forward to a new adventure.

At WSC, I started a Cougar Flying Club, keeping my pilot's license up to date. The Club members obtained a little crop-dusting plane to keep our interest and skills alive. I invited Dad up to Pullman and took him up in the plane to show him what I knew. He kept a white-knuckle grip on the door handle the entire time, became white as a sheet, and when we landed and did not say a word. I knew I had scared him.

At WSC, I met Lucia, the older sister of Eva, who I'd previously met at the library. Lucia, a schoolteacher, took some classes at WSC the summer of 1949, and we attending the same summer session. We were introduced by a mutual friend, Jeannie Campbell, who also attended WSC.

Jeannie invited me to her family home in Tieton, Washington, on the east side of the Cascade Mountains. Coincidently, Jeannie also

---

[54] Now known as Washington State University

invited Lucia to the same gathering as a guest. We found we had many mutual friends, including Lucia's sister Eva, which was a little disconcerting. It generated a rather eerie feeling when I discovered this. However, it became also joyous due to other mutual friendships. Our love grew from this foundation.

We hit it off and decided to marry on January 28, 1950. After the previous short marriage with Billie Jeanne, I wanted to make this marriage work. The GI bill allowed me to graduate WSC with a degree in psychology in 1949 and another degree in education in 1950. This time frame was an eventful one in our lives: graduation, a marriage, and a newly born son in September 1950.

In 1950, I began my teaching profession in Clarkston Washington. When I moved our family to the Seattle area in 1952, after the birth of our second son, I began teaching at Denny Junior High School for the Seattle School District that fall. I kept the student's attention by telling them war stories. I continued to serve most of my working life as a teacher or administrator for the Seattle School District. Lucia began focusing on raising our family full time.[55]

I did not attend the prestigious college my father had, nor did I have his talent for art, but I loved him dearly. He and Mother provided me the continuity and backbone I needed to succeed in the Seattle Schools. Money never became a driving force in my life; I held different values than either of my parents. They supported me in all the endeavors I attempted.

---

[55] Lucia and I now have been married for over 50 years.

TO ENDURE – REKINDLED LOVE

My father continued to work on his art. He found solace in drawing like he had his entire life. The grace of God and his artistic abilities helped to buoy him up during the Depression. His volume of artistic work spanned his lifetime and will bless the lives of generations to come. He drew places and buildings. He drew people and animals. He spent a great deal of time being precise in his work and cherished the reality and beauty of the items he drew. While others of his era took a more impressionistic tact or headed toward the neoclassical style or surrealism, Dad's work took on the realistic character of the subjects he worked with.

My father's most important works included etchings, where he etched copper plates. Generally, copper plates were covered with a waxy substance resistant to acid. He scratched through the wax to produce an image, then used an acid bath to etch images onto the copper to create the etched plate. The etched plate was inked. Then, he used the etched inked plate to press the image on to paper creating a final picture. Once sufficient prints were made, he destroyed the copper plates he etched, limiting the number of prints available for circulation. He etched bookplates, houses, buildings, landscapes and images of people in this fashion.

My father created other images of pen and ink or pencil drawings of people, places, or things. He dabbled in watercolor and oil paintings, but his labor of love continued to be the etchings. He enjoyed photography and established several memorable photo albums, but many times these photos were also translated into his etchings or drawings.

Toward the end of his life, Dad became self-reflective. He found an article written by a known columnist dated October 1950 describing

Larry Calkins

"you have what it takes." This commentary became Dad's therapy and motto for the rest of his life. The article described the courage, the friendliness and other attributes one has at sixteen years old and reminds the reader they have those attributes now. She asks the reader to remember the dreams they had and encourages them to pursue similar dreams. Additionally, she reminds the reader to be decent, brave, honest and generous. Further, mistakes should not be counted but resolves remembered instead. This morale boosting article encouraged my father to remember that anything becomes possible and he can set his mind to do it. It raised his spirits and helped him meet goals he set for himself.

Dad felt this is a good creed to have, and I agree. I refocused my life to try to live by it too.

TO ENDURE – REKINDLED LOVE

Chapter 14 – Investment Concerns

Grandmother, through her conservative, shrewd investing after my grandfather died, rebuilt her nest-egg to a small, but significant amount. Although, still modest in today's world, Grandmother did well for herself in the 1940s with the economy returning to a stable state.

In March 1949, my grandmother passed away. Joe, as the oldest child, became the executor of the Bourne estate, and he enlisted the help of his brother, Rich. Rich, previously, remained honest and straight forward, but both Joe and Rich did not fear speculation in the market place and were willing to make money however they could. The four siblings, Joe, Rich, Margaret, and young Edwin, were the beneficiaries in Grandmother's will.

Joe tried to figure out how to best utilize the funds after his mother's passing. He and Rich cooked up a scheme to aggressively build the fund into a larger nest egg for the benefit of the siblings. Of course, Joe took a commission and Rich did some work for the estate and paid himself. Both consulted my mother and their brother, Edwin, but it was obvious who benefited. My mother let her brothers run the affairs of the estate. She trusted they would attend to the best interest of the family.

Dad did not have that faith.

Mother and Dad grew through the adversity of the Depression. Both developed a strong-willed nature.

As with most married couples, the things you love about the person you've married can also be the same things that drive you crazy. For instance, Dad loved Mother's childlike mannerisms and thought her adorable. At times, she developed an innocent or naïve way of looking at life, and Dad enjoyed being able to lead when he could help her to a good solution. She, in turn, liked his strong leadership style, but those same things can be challenging.

As far as Mother's inheritance went, my father tried to provide my mother with advice on investing. He felt he could encourage and advise her in how to save and to earn money in the stock market, having years of professional experience, both successes and failures. She liked her finances the way they remained and ignored Dad's advice.

In 1953 and 1954, when the trust fund managed by her brothers expired, the brothers had not distributed the money. This infuriated Dad. He felt that the brothers, particularly Joe, took advantage of my mother. When he brought up the matter, my mother would change the subject and not discuss it. My father offered to help manage Mother's finances for her for free. He felt that Joe, Rich and the management company collected their commissions and improperly invested the funds.

TO ENDURE – REKINDLED LOVE

Evidently, Joe developed a speculation scheme with a fellow named Fox, and they expected big dollars to roll back to the family. It did not. Joe promised to make it right but did not follow through.

Between 1950 and 1953, John Fox. The owner of a Boston newspaper, "wheeled and dealed" with bonds and got in trouble with the US Tax Court. When asked how he purchased the bonds, he told the court that Joe, a successful investor, approached him.

> On my insistence, Mother wrote to Boston *(Financial Management Group)* asking for the present list of holdings and her present value of her share. They turned her letter over to Joe and he got the list of stocks, etc. with the statement that her share was …17%…. Why the reduction from approximately $150 per quarter to $66 and then back to $146? Well, when Rich came up to LA as he does occasionally, I put the question to him. He said that Joe knew a very successful speculation in New York, a Mr. Fox, who had gotten him in a speculation in "Puts and Calls" when you put up a cash margin to buy it back 100 shares. That person had gotten him the same deal and it hadn't come out quite as Fox had promised. But they expected it would. And in the meantime the $66 check was a mistake and Joe would make it up personally, but he never did. So your mother was gypped out of $100 as was Edwin. Mother said she would take it up with Joe when in New York, but she was so royally entertained by Joe and Sylvia at Nonquitt, that she didn't have any chance to see Joe alone.
>
> *1954 Letter to me from my Father*

Fox told the court, "To put it crudely, but succinctly and accurately, he (Joe) said 'I can show you how to make a bundle of money without much risk, with some possible tax benefits. Are you interested?'" Fox threw Joe under the proverbial bus.

Fox had readily agreed. Evidently, Fox had borrowed all the money he invested in the deal. Joe set it up for him by obtaining his share from others so that Fox would not have to put up any money himself but could still benefit. Obviously, some of the money Joe used was money from the siblings' inheritance.

Dad could not shake his bitter feelings over his relationships with his father-in-law. When Joe exhibited similar traits of his father, it exacerbated the bitter feelings.

***

The next year, in 1955, I received a letter from Dad marked CONIFIDENTIAL. It contained explanations of complaints of his unresolved issue with my mother. Mother wanted to throw a party for her staff at Bullocks. She had become a buyer at the store and had several sales women working for her. My mother felt the "girls" that worked with her deserved this gathering, and she wanted my father to help pay for the venue, decorations and gifts that were to be presented at the party. Dad thought it ridiculous and wanted to set some realistic parameters on my mother's plans. Mother couldn't understand why Dad couldn't liquidate some of his stocks to cover the costs of the party. But Dad had expenses of his own and explained that he didn't plan to liquidate stocks to "support her request." He also felt that the Bourne influence presented itself when she demanded payment, and, then in a fit of anger, told him to move out. As severe as these impasses appeared, they, eventually, worked through the disagreements. Both didn't like the stubbornness of the other and began to look more closely at themselves.

The compromise resulted in a scaled back party; Dad would stay in the house, and compromises would be made regarding unrelated household duties. Dad kept his stocks, but agreed to help fund some of

TO ENDURE – REKINDLED LOVE

my mother's needs. Mother held her party and the issue was resolved.

While rifts like this occur in normal marriage relationships, this one seemed like it might create a repeat of the separation that took place during the Depression. The marriage continued, but it took some work on both my father and my mother's part to make the marriage work.

****

Mother also wrote me about another issue discussing Dad's health. Since 1953, Dad had been seeing a doctor about heart problems. She became very concerned about him living with a heart ailment and felt she could nag him no longer. She didn't like him driving with the heart condition either. She asked me to talk to my

> I've forgotten what it was like to celebrate – I guess it was just before Pop's first heart attack and we were having fun out in the back yard. Maybe we had a barbequed hamburger or something. You'll have to gradually impress on Pop the fact that from here on out, slow and easy does it. It's not going to be safe for him to drive the car – suppose he should get an attack on the freeway. So, write him and in your immutable style give him the do's and don'ts of living with a heart. You can impress him much more than I. You're so tactful! I just blurt out what I think and it usually doesn't sit well and could only give him another attack.
>
> *Mother, 1954.*

father and support him in making some adjustments to the way he lived. As she often did with people, she buttered me up, calling me tactful. What Mother didn't realize was that I got my tact from her. She exaggerated.

***

My father and mother remained generally happy, living in California until he abruptly passed away from another heart attack on

Larry Calkins

June 16, 1960.

The same day, I immediately flew from Seattle to be with Mother and Sarah, who flew from Hawaii. We all had a good cry when we were finally together. While I could not believe it and became somewhat numb to his passing, I knew I would miss our long talks and discussions. He had confided in me about his devastation during the Depression, and I had always felt comfortable confiding in him about my family life. He told me all about his stock portfolios, the expenses he had, and how he had squeaked by. A dignified man, my father left this world with a dignified history and pedigree. Yet, the Great Depression left him, for a time, destitute and a marred individual. He regained his dignity after surviving and struggling though the long Depression, a dignity that he put back together piece by piece. It gave new meaning to "pulling yourself up by the bootstraps." Mother use to say, he would pull the bootstraps until he had no bootstraps left to pull, and then he would still pull some more. He grew to be a stronger person for going through his many struggles.

***

Based on his troubles in the 1950s, Uncle Joe continued to have legal difficulties. His plans to make a lot of money fast proved to be his downfall. In June 1961, according to the U.S. Attorney, Uncle Joe pleaded guilty over a deal with Mr.Keiser of conspiring to defraud the U.S. Government out of $155,000 of tax money. At the time, Joe, the President of a bank, and Mr. Keiser, a Broker out of Brookline, MA developed a plan. Joe used his experience as a note broker to obtain substantial tax deductions for Keizer's company, as well as ten other companies, by manipulating stock owned by John Fox, the former

TO ENDURE – REKINDLED LOVE

publisher of the Boston Post, and others. The judge fined Joe $11,000 as well as others on charges of conspiracy to evade income taxes in connection with a stock deal. According to the government, Joe became involved in a plan to purchase and sell $22,500 of Perth Amboy National Bank stock owned by John Fox and held by Cleveland Trust Company.[56]

In 1964, Joe added to his legal difficulties with another indictment. This time with two other people, for defrauding an insurance company, according to the New York District Attorney.[57] At least, unlike some, Uncle Joe admitted his guilt and accepted the government's penalty. I can respect him for that as hard as it must have been for him. Sadly, Joe died in 1965, maybe due, in part, to the stress of the legal battles.

With this information, my father may have had reason to be wary of Joe and perhaps, my mother should have allowed my father in the 1950's to manage her inheritance funds.

---

[56] The Boston Globe, Page 2, Article entitled "Financiers fined," Wednesday, June 28, 1961
[57] *The Boston Globe, Wed. Aug 12, 1964, Main Edition Page 5*

TO ENDURE – REKINDLED LOVE

EPILOGUE

My father's art legacy remains remarkable, although he never made a living at it. The Smithsonian recognized his work, and the Field Museum in Chicago published his art. He offered his art to several libraries in the Los Angeles area and became known in the Who's Who of American Artists. Art was his salvation during his life and his legacy after he passed away.

All of us are but one day away from a disaster. All it takes is a major downturn in the economy, a divorce, a motor vehicle accident, or a health problem, and we are wiped out financially and, often, emotionally. As one poet implied, I am lucky when I go down a road without being a person who is ill, a beggar, a prisoner, a destitute person or other folk who struggle with life. We are a day away, week away or a year away from losing our money or self-dignity or both. *It could happen to any of us.*

I believe, the best way to see ourselves is to take one day at a time, put one foot in front of the other, make the best of that day, and know what is important in our lives. In Dad's case, the love of family grew to be the most important. Without my father's family, his wife, his children, and his sisters, he would not have seen the other side of the Great Depression. He would have perished. Money did not save him, nor will it save us. Love did.

After Dad died, Mother, with characteristic independence, purchased a large berry farm in Silverton, Oregon, with the desire to operate as a business enterprise. Although the endeavor didn't work out, she found the mountain community of Rockport, Washington, to her liking. She found and purchased another small acreage there and then remarried. The farm life reminded her of the times during the Depression when she gardened and raised chickens in Marshfield. It seemed out of character considering her upbringing, but she liked it. Her new husband, Sam Heath, was a good choice, but she outlived her new husband by several years. Sam knew farming in the Rockport area and knew how to care for Mother's property, by clearing weeds, maintaining her pasture and fruit trees. His eyes sparkled when he was around her and she deeply appreciated his companionship. Yet, when he passed, living alone in Rockport for her was undesirable, so Mother moved to a mobile home in Kenmore, Washington to be near me. When she started to become forgetful, she spent her last days in a nursing home near Sarah in Dallas, Texas.

Margaret Howland Calkins was a singular and very special person. Her gracious and witty mannerisms accented by a pervasive charm attracting attention wherever she went. People easily recognized her self-confidence and poised demeanor, and seldom failed to want to know her better. Her seven grandchildren adored her, as did nearly all who knew her well.

Early in 1993, on my next to last visit to her nursing home, I

TO ENDURE – REKINDLED LOVE

wheeled Mother down the hall in her wheelchair, and she looked back with her head cocked so she can see my expression. She gives me a sly smile and I'm wondering all the while if she really recognizes me. She smiles at me and asks in a flirtatious way, "Do you love me?"

I wonder if this question shows recognition, or if she's just being coy with this stranger who's pushing her along. So, I answered in measured tones, "Yes, Mother. I love you." And, then I know she knows by the way she responded with much satisfaction in her voice, "Well—that's good!"

That's good, Mother. That's good.

Larry Calkins

TO ENDURE – REKINDLED LOVE

Reflections:

I told and wrote down some stories earlier in my life that capture some fun aspects of our story. Because of my dementia, I sometimes ramble as I relate these stories. For example, when I described the situation around the "Old Bastard" or the "old man", I became emotional at that time. My wife warned me with a simple, "Travis," and I knew I had overstepped my explanation. Consequently, I was thrilled when Larry asked me to help with this manuscript as I am failing in my capacity to express myself. I specifically wanted to describe the soft side of my father. When he neared the end of his life, he appeared somewhat gruff because of failing health. My immediate family knew Mother much better and loved her dearly.

My father assembled an album that told stories of his early life with my mother. I kept letters my parents wrote me of their lives in bits and pieces.

My hope, for my dear extended family and reader is that they will read this story and walk away with a better sense of who these relatives were. In addition, I hope the reader will learn from their influence and mistakes, and then live a fuller life because of their stories.

Thank you for the privilege of telling their stories.

With Love.

Travis Calkins,

Larry Calkins

ABOUT THE AUTHOR:

Larry Calkins was raised in the state of Washington. He attended a University located in Washington State. After graduation, he worked in Oregon as an Environmental Specialist. When he retired from being a state employee, Larry and his wife moved to Arizona where they currently reside.

Since retiring, Larry became interested in his family history, longed to understand his family's roots and to understand family members as individuals. This desire prompted him to write a book like this one. Other books written or published by Larry Calkins include:

The Journal -
>By Emma Bourne

Loring Gary Calkins Senior Art Work
>A pictorial essay

www.ingramcontent.com/pod-product-compliance
Lightning Source LLC
Chambersburg PA
CBHW060153050426
42446CB00013B/2808